The Unholy Unions

The Popes, Their Mistresses, and Illegitimate Heirs

A.A. Castor

Table of Contents

The Unholy Unions: The Popes, Their Mistresses, and Illegitimate Heirs

A.A. Castor

A.A. Castor

Dedication

To my beloved family,

Your unconditional love, unwavering support, and endless encouragement have been my greatest blessings. From the earliest days of dreaming to the challenging moments of writing, you have stood by me with patience and belief. This book is as much yours as it is mine, a reflection of the values you've instilled and the faith you've shown in me. Thank you for being my rock and my inspiration.

To my dear friends,

Your friendship has illuminated my path with laughter, shared moments, and invaluable support. You've cheered me on through every triumph and lifted me up through every challenge. Your belief in my endeavors has been a source of strength and motivation. This book is a testament to the power of friendship, and I am grateful for each of you who has walked this journey by my side.

To God,

Your grace and guidance have been my constant companions. In moments of doubt, you've shown me the way; in moments of joy, you've multiplied my gratitude. This book is a testament to your faithfulness and the blessings you've bestowed upon me. May it serve as a reflection of your love and the lessons you continue to teach me.

With heartfelt gratitude and love,

A.A. Castor

Copyright © 2024 by A.A. Castor

Why I Am Writing This Book

When I first began to delve into the history of the papacy, I was searching for answers to the questions that had long fascinated me: How could men who were entrusted with the spiritual leadership of millions, who held the keys to heaven and the responsibility for guiding souls, fall so deeply into scandal, corruption, and moral compromise? The more I studied, the more I realized that these popes, while wielding immense power, were not so different from the kings, emperors, and noblemen of their time. They were driven by the same ambitions, the same hunger for power, the same desire to leave a legacy. But what set them apart was their unique position—the papacy.

As I read through centuries of history, I found stories that seemed almost too unbelievable to be true: Popes who fathered children, appointed their sons as cardinals, and sold church offices to the highest bidder. Popes who manipulated the marriages of their daughters to forge alliances with powerful families, who dined with their mistresses in the halls of the Vatican, and whose actions were so brazen that they came to symbolize the very corruption they were supposed to fight. And yet, these weren't just men of scandal—they were men of history, shaping the course of Europe in ways both seen and unseen.

I began to see a thread running through these stories, one that connected the political power plays of the Renaissance with the moral dilemmas of the papacy. The more I learned about figures like **Pope Alexander VI, Pope Innocent VIII**, and the infamous **Borgia family**, the more I saw that the papacy, at its core, was not just a spiritual office—it was a throne in the heart of Europe, a seat of power as coveted and contested as any kingdom.

As I dug deeper, I realized that this story wasn't just about individual popes; it was about the **institution of the papacy itself**—how it straddled the line between the spiritual and the temporal, between heaven and earth. It was a tale of ambition, loyalty, betrayal, and survival. These popes weren't just historical figures—they were characters in a drama of epic proportions, each one playing their part in the shaping of the Church and the world.

I knew then that this was a story that needed to be told—not in dry academic terms, but as a living, breathing account of power and corruption, of family and faith, of the very human desires that shaped one of the most powerful institutions in the world.

I am writing this book because, at its heart, it is a **human story**. It's about the men who sat on the throne of St. Peter, not as saints but as flawed, ambitious individuals who struggled with the same temptations as any other rulers of their time. Their actions, both scandalous and strategic, shaped the course of history in ways that still resonate today.

By writing this book, I hope to pull back the curtain on the papacy during its most turbulent periods and invite readers into a world where spiritual authority met political ambition. It's a world where popes were not just religious figures but political power brokers, military strategists, and, at times, deeply flawed men driven by personal and familial desires.

I want readers to be fascinated, shocked, and perhaps even empathetic toward these historical figures. Because, in the end, the history of the papacy is a story about people—about their ambitions, their struggles, and their complex humanity. And it's a story that, despite the centuries that have passed, still has the power to captivate and compel us today.

So, join me on this journey through the corridors of the Vatican, the battlefields of Italy, and the courts of Europe, where popes shaped history not only with prayers but with politics, power, and scandal. This is why I am writing this book—because the story of these popes is, in many ways, the story of us all.

Warning and Disclaimer

The information contained in this book is provided for educational and informational purposes only. The author and publisher have made every effort to ensure the accuracy of the information provided herein, but the contents of this book are not guaranteed to be free of errors or omissions. The author and publisher accept no responsibility or liability for any loss or damage, whether direct, indirect, or consequential, that may result from the use or misuse of the information contained within this book.

This book is not intended to provide professional advice or services. Readers should seek the assistance of qualified professionals before making any decisions based on the information presented in this book.

The author and publisher disclaim any and all liability arising from actions taken or not taken based on the content of this book. The author and publisher make no warranties, expressed or implied, regarding the fitness or appropriateness of the information contained within for any particular purpose.

By reading and using this book, you acknowledge that you understand and agree to this disclaimer and that the author and publisher are not liable for any outcomes or consequences resulting from the use of the information contained herein.

About the Author

A.A. Castor is a dedicated writer and researcher with a passion for exploring the intersections of **history**, **leadership**, and **power**. With a focus on uncovering the human stories behind great historical figures, Castor delves into the motivations, scandals, and ambitions that shaped some of the most powerful individuals in world history. His work spans topics from political strategy and philosophy to religious history and social dynamics.

Castor's deep interest in the papacy and its role in shaping Europe led him to write about some of the most controversial and notorious popes in history, particularly those who used their spiritual office to pursue personal and familial ambition. His writing seeks to understand the complex forces at play in the lives of these individuals—how they navigated the delicate balance between **spiritual authority** and **worldly power**.

Beyond writing, Castor hosts a podcast that explores leadership, historical events, and the timeless lessons they offer for today's challenges. His research and work draw readers into the heart of pivotal moments in history, offering new perspectives on the figures who shaped the world we live in.

A.A. Castor's commitment to meticulous research and compelling storytelling brings history to life, allowing readers to connect with the past in ways that resonate with the present. Whether examining the scandals of the Renaissance papacy or exploring the philosophical underpinnings of leadership, Castor's work offers deep insights into the motivations that drive individuals in positions of power.

Introduction

Throughout history, the papacy has been regarded as the epitome of spiritual authority, moral leadership, and divine guidance for millions of Christians worldwide. The Pope, revered as the "Holy Father," stands at the head of the Catholic Church, embodying piety, discipline, and a commitment to God. Yet, behind the gilded doors of the Vatican, not all pontiffs have lived in strict accordance with these sacred ideals.

In this book, **"The Unholy Unions: The Popes, Their Mistresses, and Illegitimate Heirs,"** we delve into one of the most controversial and lesser-known aspects of the papacy—those popes who, despite their vows of celibacy, pursued illicit relationships and fathered children. These stories are not simply about the indiscretions of powerful men but serve as a window into an era when the lines between spiritual leadership and worldly ambition were often blurred, and the consequences of these unions extended far beyond the walls of the Vatican.

The Catholic Church, particularly in its earlier centuries, was rife with political maneuvering, corruption, and scandal. Popes who fathered illegitimate heirs through mistresses or secret marriages wielded their spiritual and temporal power not just for the Church's benefit, but also to secure the futures of their families. Sons were elevated to princely ranks or even future papacies, while daughters were married into noble families to strengthen the Church's political alliances.

From Pope Alexander VI, whose Borgia family name became synonymous with corruption and excess, to the lesser-known Pope Sergius III, whose affair with a powerful Roman noblewoman led to the birth of a future pope, this book uncovers the forbidden passions, dynastic schemes, and moral failings that have been carefully obscured in the annals of papal history.

We will explore how these popes navigated their dual roles—managing both the Church's spiritual needs and the worldly desires of their personal lives. How did they justify their behavior, often flaunting Church doctrine, while maintaining power and control? How did their secret unions and illegitimate children shape the course of Church history, and what impact did these scandalous relationships have on the Catholic faith?

Through their stories, we confront an uncomfortable truth: that even those in positions of the highest moral authority are not immune to the temptations of power, lust, and family ambition. Yet, it is precisely these human frailties that make their tales so compelling, as they reveal the complex interplay between divine duty and earthly desire.

This is a history of the papacy as you've never heard it before—one of hidden lovers, forbidden offspring, and dynastic ambitions that, for centuries, shaped the course of Western history. Welcome to **"The Unholy Unions,"** where the spiritual and the scandalous meet, and the Vatican's darkest secrets are laid bare.

1. Pope Adrian II (867–872)

Life and Background

Pope Adrian II's rise to the papacy was marked by a combination of his deep involvement in Church affairs and an unusual personal history for someone who would ascend to the highest spiritual office in the Catholic Church. Born into a prominent Roman noble family around 792, Adrian had long been connected to the ecclesiastical world, but unlike many of his papal predecessors and successors, he was not bound by clerical celibacy for most of his life. Before becoming pope, Adrian had married and fathered children, which set him apart from the norm even in a time when the rules of celibacy were not yet fully enforced. His family life would continue to follow him into his papal career, making his reign distinct in more ways than one.

At the time of his election to the papacy in 867, Adrian II was already an elderly man, believed to be around 75 years old. His election was a compromise between different factions in the Church, seeking a neutral and respected figure to lead them after the death of Pope Nicholas I. Adrian had been passed over twice before for the papacy, and now in his advanced age, his long years of service and reputation for piety finally secured him the position. However, unlike most of his predecessors, Adrian brought with him not just his clerical experience but also his family, a wife and daughter, who would live with him during his papacy.

Adrian's decision to keep his wife and daughter close after assuming the papacy raised eyebrows in some circles, although it did not create outright scandal. At the time, the Church's requirement for clerical celibacy was still in transition, not yet strictly enforced across all ranks of the clergy. It was not entirely uncommon for clergy members to have families, particularly if they had been married before ordination, as was the case with Adrian. Nevertheless, the image of the pope, the supreme spiritual leader of Christendom, living with a wife and child at the Lateran Palace stood out and became a significant part of his legacy. This was a time when the tension between the rising ideal of celibacy and the traditional practices of clerics having families was still being resolved within the Church.

Adrian's background as a family man reflected this evolving tension. While many church leaders saw celibacy as a virtuous ideal that should be adopted by all members of the clergy, it was still not fully implemented at the time of Adrian's election. Previous popes had also been married before joining the clergy, but Adrian was unique in that his family life remained public knowledge throughout his time as pope. His wife, Stephania, and their daughter were often present at papal gatherings, further emphasizing his unconventional status.

In many ways, Pope Adrian II's personal life also intersected with his political and religious duties. His marriage, while not scandalous in a traditional sense, highlighted the changing nature of Church leadership. His papacy came during a time of great political upheaval, as Adrian struggled to maintain peace between warring factions in Italy and beyond. Yet, it was his family ties that remained a point of curiosity. It is worth noting that Adrian's personal background did not seem to impede his ability to perform his papal duties. In fact, he continued the efforts of his predecessors in maintaining the Church's spiritual authority, mediating between secular rulers, and promoting unity within the Church.

However, tragedy struck Adrian II's family during his time as pope. His daughter was abducted and murdered by Eleutherius, the brother of Anastasius the Librarian, an influential figure in Rome at the time.

The event cast a dark shadow over Adrian's papacy and deeply affected him on a personal level. This tragic loss may have further complicated Adrian's relationship with the Vatican elite, as it exposed the dangers and intrigues of Roman political life. The murder of his daughter underscored the volatility of the period and the personal toll that such a high office could take on its occupant. Despite his advanced age and personal suffering, Adrian continued his papal duties, though his reign was not marked by any major theological or political achievements.

Adrian's personal story, that of a husband and father while sitting on the papal throne, gave him a unique place in the history of the papacy. He serves as an example of how the early medieval papacy was still grappling with the enforcement of clerical celibacy and how personal and family life could intersect with spiritual leadership. While his tenure as pope was relatively short, his personal circumstances continue to make him a subject of interest for those studying the history of the Church. His papacy is a reminder that the leaders of the Church, even in their roles as spiritual guides, were often deeply entangled in the familial, social, and political realities of their time.

Scandals and Exploits

THE DECISION OF POPE Adrian II to maintain his family within the walls of the papal residence during his reign was one of the most unusual and controversial aspects of his papacy. At a time when clerical celibacy was not yet strictly enforced, but increasingly idealized, Adrian's choice to live openly with his wife and daughter at the Lateran Palace caused both surprise and discomfort within ecclesiastical circles. While not considered outright scandalous by the standards of the era, this situation was certainly controversial, as it stood in contrast to the growing expectations of celibate clergy, particularly for someone holding the highest office in the Church.

During the 9th century, the Church was still in the process of transitioning towards a more rigid enforcement of celibacy, particularly for the higher clergy. Pope Adrian II, having been married before his ordination, was technically within the bounds of what was permissible at the time. However, the optics of the pope—God's representative on Earth—living alongside his wife, Stephania, and daughter presented a curious image. It was especially notable because the papacy was becoming more closely associated with ideals of spiritual purity, which included celibacy as a defining characteristic.

Adrian's decision to retain his family during his papacy could be interpreted in various ways. On one hand, it might reflect his belief that family life did not inherently conflict with his role as a spiritual leader. Adrian, by all accounts, was a devout and pious man who had lived a life of service to the Church, and his commitment to his family may have been seen by some as an expression of his moral values. On the other hand, there was certainly discomfort within some segments of the Church hierarchy, as the presence of a pope's wife and daughter within the Vatican added an element of domesticity to the papal household that clashed with the growing emphasis on clerical separation from worldly attachments.

This tension, while not erupting into a full-blown scandal, did raise concerns. The Church had long been working to solidify its authority, not only in spiritual matters but also in terms of setting an example for Christian society. The ideal of celibacy was being promoted as a symbol of devotion and purity, and Adrian's situation complicated this narrative. While some clergy, particularly in the Eastern Church, had historically been married, the Roman Catholic Church was pushing towards a more rigid enforcement of celibate discipline, especially for those in leadership positions. Adrian's personal life therefore became a subject of both curiosity and mild controversy.

Moreover, there were practical concerns as well. By keeping his wife and daughter close, Adrian may have inadvertently opened himself up to accusations of nepotism or favoritism, although there is little historical evidence to suggest that he used his papal power to benefit his family. However, the mere presence of his family in the papal residence could have fueled suspicions, particularly in a time when political and familial ties often influenced Church appointments and decisions. In a city like Rome, where power struggles between noble families and the Church were common, the optics of a pope maintaining a family could be seen as problematic by some factions.

The greatest tragedy, however, came when Adrian's daughter was abducted and murdered by Eleutherius, the brother of Anastasius the Librarian, an influential figure in Rome at the time. This event added a deeply personal and dramatic element to the controversy surrounding Adrian's papacy. The abduction and murder of his daughter were not just a personal loss but a political incident that shocked Rome. It highlighted the vulnerability and instability of even the highest leaders in the city and brought to light the dangers of allowing family matters to intersect with the intense political intrigues surrounding the papacy.

While Adrian II did not face the type of moral outrage or ecclesiastical backlash that later popes with families would experience, the presence of his wife and daughter at the Lateran Palace was unusual enough to draw attention. It reflected a time of transition in the Church, where the enforcement of celibacy was becoming a more central issue, and it illustrated the complexities of balancing personal life with spiritual duties at the highest level of the Church.

In retrospect, Adrian's decision to keep his family close can be seen as both a personal and political choice, one that demonstrated his commitment to his loved ones while simultaneously creating a subtle but significant controversy in the context of the evolving norms of clerical celibacy. His reign as pope, though relatively short and devoid of major theological disputes, remains notable for this unique aspect of his papal life, highlighting the intersection of personal and spiritual obligations in a way that few other popes have had to navigate.

Corruption

WHILE POPE ADRIAN II'S papacy was not marked by overt scandals of corruption, his unique position as a married man with a family living alongside him during his tenure did raise some concerns, particularly regarding perceptions of nepotism or favoritism. During this era, the papacy was not just a spiritual office; it also wielded significant political and social influence, and any hint of personal gain or favoritism could tarnish a pope's legacy. Adrian's papacy occurred in a period where the balance between spiritual duty and familial obligations often blurred the lines of clerical conduct, leading to quiet questions about the propriety of his family ties.

Unlike some of his predecessors or successors, Adrian II does not appear to have been heavily involved in acts of nepotism or personal enrichment. However, the mere presence of his wife and daughter at the Lateran Palace during his papacy created an unusual situation that drew attention. The possibility of favoritism toward family members, especially in a city rife with political intrigue, was a concern. Rome in the 9th century was a place where power struggles between the Church and noble families were common, and the potential for any pope to use his position to elevate family members or secure their future was always a looming issue.

Adrian's predecessor, Pope Nicholas I, had established a legacy of strong moral authority and reform, and expectations for the papacy were high. Adrian II, being a married pope, faced the challenge of maintaining the dignity of the papal office while navigating the delicate situation of his family's presence. There is little evidence that Adrian used his position to unduly promote his family, but the very fact that his wife, Stephania, and daughter lived openly with him created an atmosphere of suspicion in some quarters.

The most significant event related to his family during his papacy was the tragic abduction and murder of his daughter by Eleutherius, the brother of Anastasius the Librarian, a prominent Roman figure. This incident brought to light the vulnerability of Adrian's family, but it also stirred controversy. The murder raised questions about whether Adrian's family ties had somehow become entangled with the political rivalries of the time, though there is no direct evidence that Adrian's actions or decisions as pope were compromised by this personal loss.

Nevertheless, the fact that such a violent act could occur within the pope's immediate family highlighted the volatility of Roman politics during Adrian's reign. The tragic event demonstrated that even the pope's family could not escape the dangers of living in a politically charged environment where the lines between personal and political grievances were often blurred. Some may have speculated that Adrian's decision to maintain his family so close to the seat of power made them targets, though this is more a reflection of the time's violent political climate than any direct corruption on Adrian's part.

Adrian's contemporaries did not view his papacy as particularly corrupt compared to other more infamous pontificates. He largely continued the policies of his predecessor, Pope Nicholas I, focusing on maintaining the Church's moral authority and mediating disputes between secular rulers. However, his papacy lacked the sweeping reforms or strong moral leadership of Nicholas, and it could be said that Adrian's reign was somewhat overshadowed by the unusual circumstances of his family life. His tenure as pope was not characterized by major doctrinal or political initiatives, which may explain why accusations of corruption, nepotism, or favoritism never fully took hold.

In the end, Pope Adrian II's papacy does not stand out as one of corruption or overt misuse of power, but rather as a period in which the personal intersected with the spiritual in ways that caused discomfort for some within the Church. His family's presence, while not leading to overt acts of favoritism, nevertheless created a situation where concerns about nepotism were possible, even if they did not manifest into any clear accusations. Adrian's papacy reflects a time when the papal office was still grappling with the enforcement of celibacy and the complexities of familial ties in a role that demanded spiritual purity and focus.

Handling His Family

POPE ADRIAN II'S PAPACY stands out in the history of the Church due to the unusual circumstance of having a wife and daughter present during his reign. Balancing his familial responsibilities while serving as the leader of the Catholic Church created a unique dynamic that few popes had to navigate, particularly as celibacy was becoming more firmly established as a key expectation for Church leaders. However, despite these challenges, Adrian II appears to have managed this delicate situation with a sense of duty both to his family and to the Church.

Adrian's decision to keep his wife, Stephania, and their daughter by his side at the Lateran Palace was remarkable for the time, as popes, bishops, and other clergy were increasingly expected to model celibate lives. While Adrian had been married long before becoming pope and thus was not breaking any rules that applied to his particular case, the optics of the pope, who was seen as the highest moral authority in Christendom, living with his family, may have caused discomfort among certain Church officials and observers. Nevertheless, Adrian's family ties seem to have had little direct impact on his ability to perform his papal duties.

As an elderly man at the time of his election, Adrian may have felt that separating from his family was neither necessary nor appropriate, particularly as he had lived with them throughout his long service to the Church prior to becoming pope. His bond with his family was clearly important to him, and he did not attempt to hide them from public view, allowing them to remain close even as he assumed the immense responsibilities of leading the Catholic Church. This choice may have also reflected Adrian's more personal and pragmatic approach to his papacy, focusing less on conforming to the emerging ideals of celibacy and more on maintaining his longstanding role as both a husband and father.

While Adrian II was certainly dedicated to his spiritual duties, his familial responsibilities appeared to carry significant weight. His wife and daughter continued to live with him, and by all accounts, he managed to balance both his public and private lives without too much disruption. The fact that his family resided at the papal palace indicates that Adrian made no effort to conceal his domestic life from the Church or the Roman public. This openness suggests that Adrian likely viewed his family as a source of stability and support, even as he took on the highest role in Christendom.

However, his papacy would be marred by the tragic murder of his daughter, which brought the tension between his family life and his public role to the forefront. His daughter's abduction and murder by Eleutherius, the brother of Anastasius the Librarian, shocked the Roman public and devastated Adrian. This tragedy highlighted the dangers of maintaining a family in such a politically volatile environment, where personal conflicts could easily escalate into violence. Despite the tragedy, Adrian remained steadfast in his papal duties, continuing to lead the Church and navigate its complex relationship with secular rulers.

The way Adrian handled this tragedy speaks to his resilience as both a father and a pope. Though personally devastated, he did not allow the incident to derail his papacy. Instead, he continued to carry out his responsibilities, albeit with the weight of personal loss. This balance between his role as the head of the Church and his identity as a husband and father demonstrates Adrian's ability to manage both spheres of his life, even under the most trying circumstances.

Overall, Adrian II's ability to balance his duties as a pope with his familial obligations speaks to his personal strength and his ability to navigate a complex and often difficult situation. His papacy may not have been marked by major theological or political reforms, but it stands out as an example of how a pope could manage the personal and spiritual dimensions of his life simultaneously. While some within the Church may have viewed his family's presence with unease, Adrian's dedication to both his family and the Church remained evident throughout his reign. His legacy, though tinged with tragedy, reflects a man who sought to uphold his responsibilities in both arenas, navigating the unique challenges that came with being a pope with a family.

2. Pope Sergius III (904–911)

Life and Background

Pope Sergius III's rise to power is set against one of the most tumultuous and scandal-ridden periods in the history of the papacy, often referred to as the "Saeculum Obscurum" or "Dark Age of the Papacy." Born into a noble Roman family around 860, Sergius was well-positioned for a career in the Church. His aristocratic connections helped him ascend the clerical ranks, and he became a bishop before he was even forty, which was relatively young for such a position at the time.

Sergius' early career was deeply entangled with the political power struggles of Rome. In the late 9th and early 10th centuries, the papacy was heavily influenced by various noble families, particularly the powerful Theophylact family, which played a decisive role in determining who would hold the papal throne. Sergius was initially elected pope in 898, but his claim was quickly contested. His brief early papacy was cut short due to the political turmoil surrounding the papal office, forcing him into exile when Pope John IX replaced him.

Despite his exile, Sergius maintained his political ambitions, aligning himself with influential Roman factions that supported his claim to the papal throne. His fortunes changed when he secured the favor of **Marozia**, the daughter of Theophylact, who became one of the most powerful and influential women in Roman politics. Marozia, a noblewoman with deep political ties, played a pivotal role in the complex power dynamics of the time and wielded significant influence over the papal elections.

It is widely believed that Sergius and Marozia became lovers, a relationship that had both personal and political ramifications. Marozia's support helped secure Sergius' return to power in 904 when he was reinstalled as pope through force, backed by her family's military and political strength. The nature of their relationship was more than just a political alliance; it is also believed that Sergius fathered a child with Marozia, a boy who would later become **Pope John XI**.

Sergius' relationship with Marozia played a significant role in his rise to power, as her family essentially controlled the papacy during this period. Their liaison became part of the larger narrative of the corruption and moral decay of the Church at that time, with the papacy often being treated as a pawn in the power games of Rome's noble families. Marozia's influence extended beyond her romantic ties to Sergius, as she would continue to shape the politics of the Church for years to come through her descendants and her manipulation of papal elections.

Once in power, Sergius III wasted no time consolidating his position. His papacy was marked by brutality and the elimination of his rivals. One of his first acts as pope was to reverse the decrees of his predecessor, Pope Formosus, whom Sergius had long despised. He ordered the exhumation and desecration of Formosus' body, a posthumous trial that symbolized the brutal and vengeful nature of Sergius' reign.

Although Sergius III's papacy is remembered for its violent and corrupt nature, his relationship with Marozia stands out as one of the more scandalous aspects of his time as pope. Their affair, though never officially acknowledged by the Church, became a well-known episode in the historical accounts of the period. Sergius and Marozia's child,

John XI, would go on to become pope in 931, further entrenching the Theophylact family's influence over the Church.

Sergius III's life and rise to the papacy, therefore, are emblematic of the broader decline in moral and spiritual authority that characterized the Church in the 10th century. His career was shaped by political machinations, ruthless ambition, and the manipulation of papal power by influential Roman families. The shadow of his relationship with Marozia looms large over his legacy, intertwining the personal with the political in a way that would leave a lasting stain on the papacy for decades to come.

Scandals and Exploits

ONE OF THE MOST NOTORIOUS and enduring scandals of Pope Sergius III's papacy was his intimate involvement with **Marozia**, a powerful Roman noblewoman, and his alleged fathering of a future pope, **John XI**. This scandal became one of the central stories of the "Saeculum Obscurum" or "The Dark Age of the Papacy," a period marked by corruption, intrigue, and the manipulation of the papal office by influential Roman families. Sergius III's affair with Marozia not only tainted his personal reputation but also cast a long shadow over the papacy itself, solidifying its place as a tool of political power rather than a purely spiritual office during this era.

Marozia was the daughter of **Theophylact of Tusculum**, a powerful Roman senator and ruler, who, along with his wife Theodora, effectively controlled Rome and had significant influence over the election of popes. Marozia herself was a skilled manipulator of political power, and her involvement with Sergius III helped her family cement their grip on the papacy. The relationship between Sergius and Marozia was not just a romantic liaison but also a strategic alliance that benefitted both parties.

Their affair, however, led to one of the most scandalous outcomes in papal history—the birth of their son, **John**, who would later become **Pope John XI**. Although the Church has never officially confirmed Sergius III's paternity, many historians agree that John XI was almost certainly the son of Sergius and Marozia. This connection, if true, would make Sergius III the only pope known to have fathered another pope, a scandal that contributed to the image of a morally compromised papacy during this period.

The circumstances surrounding this scandal highlight the deep entanglement of the papacy with Roman aristocracy and the willingness of these families to exploit the Church for personal and political gain. Sergius III's relationship with Marozia was emblematic of the period's disregard for the spiritual sanctity of the office. Rather than focusing on religious leadership or moral authority, the papacy had become a pawn in the hands of the Theophylact family, with Marozia and her family wielding significant power behind the scenes.

Marozia's control over Sergius III during his papacy was well-documented, and she continued to play a pivotal role in Rome's political landscape long after Sergius' death. Her manipulation of the papacy was most clearly demonstrated when her son, John XI, was elevated to the papal office in 931, long after Sergius' reign. As pope, John XI was often considered to be under Marozia's influence, further solidifying her family's control over the Vatican.

Sergius III's involvement in this scandal marked a sharp decline in the moral standing of the papacy. His flagrant disregard for clerical celibacy and the deeply personal connection to one of Rome's most powerful and controversial noblewomen made his papacy a symbol of corruption. Unlike some popes who engaged in clandestine affairs, Sergius III's relationship with Marozia was an open secret, and the resulting birth of John XI only amplified the controversy.

Additionally, Sergius' reign itself was marked by ruthless violence and corruption, including the infamous "Cadaver Synod," in which the body of his rival, Pope Formosus, was exhumed and placed on trial posthumously. Sergius played a role in this macabre event, reversing Formosus' decisions and tarnishing the reputation of the Church even further. His violent consolidation of power and alliance with Marozia's family during this period of instability only added to the aura of scandal that surrounded his papacy.

In conclusion, Pope Sergius III's affair with Marozia and the birth of their son, John XI, became one of the defining scandals of his reign. This relationship showcased the deeply politicized and morally compromised nature of the papacy during the 10th century, and it remains a pivotal example of the way in which personal relationships and power struggles shaped the direction of the Church. Sergius III's legacy, therefore, is forever intertwined with the exploits of Marozia and the shadowy rule of Rome's aristocratic families over the papacy.

Corruption

POPE SERGIUS III'S papacy was deeply enmeshed in the political corruption of early 10th-century Rome, a period during which the papacy became a battleground for the city's most powerful aristocratic families. Sergius' close alliance with the **Theophylact family**, one of the most dominant Roman dynasties of the time, was both the source of his power and the root of the corruption that characterized his reign. The Theophylacts, led by **Theophylact of Tusculum** and his wife, **Theodora**, wielded immense influence over the city of Rome and the papacy, using it as a tool to expand their political control.

Sergius' rise to the papacy was largely orchestrated by the Theophylact family, whose support was crucial in securing his position as pope after a period of political instability. In the late 9th and early 10th centuries, the papacy had become a prize for Roman noble families who sought to extend their power over both the Church and the city. The Theophylacts were among the most powerful of these families, controlling large swathes of Rome and manipulating the selection of popes to suit their own interests.

Sergius III's previous attempt at the papacy in 898 had been short-lived, but with the backing of the Theophylacts, he was able to seize the papal throne again in 904 through violent means. Supported by their military strength and political clout, Sergius deposed the sitting Pope Leo V and had the antipope Christopher imprisoned, clearing his path to power. This ruthless consolidation of power was a clear sign of the corrupt nature of his alliance with the Theophylacts, as the papacy became a means to achieve political domination rather than spiritual leadership.

Once installed as pope, Sergius III effectively became a puppet of the Theophylact family, particularly of Theophylact's daughter, **Marozia**, with whom he had a well-known relationship. The Theophylacts exercised control over Rome's political and religious affairs, using Sergius as their instrument to further their influence. This period saw the papacy degraded into a tool for securing family power, with Sergius acting more as a figurehead for the Theophylacts' ambitions than as a spiritual leader.

The implications of this alliance were far-reaching. Sergius' papacy marked a continuation of the trend in which noble families treated the papal office as a personal asset to be manipulated for their own advantage. Nepotism and favoritism became rampant, as positions within the Church were awarded based on loyalty to the Theophylacts rather than merit. This corruption extended beyond the walls of the Vatican, affecting the governance of Rome and the broader influence of the Church. The papacy's reputation as a moral and spiritual authority was severely undermined as it became clear that the office was controlled by a single, powerful Roman family.

One of the most infamous acts of Sergius III's papacy, which further highlighted the corruption of the period, was his role in the **Cadaver Synod**. This grotesque event, in which the body of Pope Formosus was exhumed and put on trial, had occurred before Sergius became pope, but Sergius played a key role in continuing the vendetta against Formosus. Upon regaining power, Sergius overturned Formosus' ordinations and officially condemned his papacy. The act was not just a personal vendetta but also a move to cement the Theophylact family's control over the Church by erasing the legacy of a rival pope.

The Theophylact family's influence over the papacy continued well beyond Sergius III's reign, as their manipulation of Church affairs set a precedent for subsequent popes. After Sergius, their control remained strong, and Marozia's influence in particular grew as she later orchestrated the election of her son, John XI, to the papacy, further embedding the family's power within the Church. Sergius' complicity in this system of corruption marked a low point in the history of the papacy, where the moral and spiritual leadership of the Church was subverted by political and familial ambitions.

The corruption of Sergius III's papacy serves as a prime example of how deeply entangled the papacy became with the political and aristocratic power structures of Rome during the "Dark Age of the Papacy." His reign, heavily influenced by his alliance with the Theophylact family, was defined by the subordination of spiritual responsibilities to political objectives. This corruption tarnished the reputation of the papacy and contributed to the broader decline of the Church's moral authority during this period, leaving a legacy of intrigue, power struggles, and manipulation that would take centuries to fully repair.

Handling His Family

POPE SERGIUS III'S relationship with Marozia, a powerful Roman noblewoman, and their alleged son, **John XI**, played a significant role in shaping his papacy. This familial connection exemplified how the personal relationships of popes during this era could deeply intertwine with the political machinations of Rome, often to the detriment of the Church's spiritual integrity. Sergius III's handling of his family was, in many ways, a reflection of the era's pervasive corruption, where papal authority was frequently subordinated to personal ambition and family alliances.

Marozia, the daughter of the influential **Theophylact of Tusculum**, was not just a romantic partner for Sergius III but also a key figure in his rise to power. Their relationship, more than just personal, was deeply political. Marozia's family, particularly her father and mother, controlled much of Rome's political and military power, and their support was critical in helping Sergius regain the papal throne in 904. Marozia, already a skilled political operator, leveraged her influence to secure Sergius' position as pope, and in return, Sergius allowed her family unprecedented control over papal affairs.

Sergius III's relationship with Marozia became one of the most scandalous aspects of his papacy, particularly because of the birth of their son, **John**, who would later become **Pope John XI**. While the Church never officially confirmed Sergius III's paternity, many contemporary sources and later historians believe that John XI was indeed Sergius' son, a fact that further fueled the perception of Sergius as a morally compromised leader. The implications of fathering a future pope were far-reaching, as it demonstrated the extent to which familial ties and personal relationships could manipulate the highest office in Christendom.

Maintaining this relationship with Marozia during his papacy required careful balancing on Sergius' part. Marozia's power and influence in Rome meant that Sergius had to ensure her continued favor, not just as a lover but also as a political ally. Their relationship, while beneficial to Sergius in consolidating his control over the papacy, also came with its own challenges. By allowing Marozia such influence over Church affairs, Sergius effectively became a puppet to the Theophylact family, particularly Marozia, whose ambitions extended beyond merely supporting Sergius. Her ultimate goal was to maintain her family's dominance over the Vatican and Roman politics, and Sergius' papacy served as a means to achieve that.

Sergius III's son, John, became a key figure in the later political maneuverings of Marozia. After Sergius' death, Marozia ensured that John XI, still a young man, was elevated to the papal office in 931. This appointment was a clear demonstration of the power that the Theophylact family continued to wield over the papacy. Sergius III's handling of his family thus extended beyond his lifetime, as his familial ties laid the groundwork for his son to follow in his footsteps, further entrenching the family's control over the Church. John XI's papacy, like Sergius', was marred by the dominance of Marozia, who effectively ruled Rome through her son.

Sergius' relationship with his family influenced not only the politics of the Vatican but also the broader perception of the papacy during this era. His decision to maintain close ties with Marozia and their son exemplified how deeply intertwined the papal office had become with Roman aristocracy and personal interests. The moral authority of the pope was significantly undermined by these relationships, as it became clear that familial loyalty and political ambition often took precedence over spiritual leadership.

Sergius III's handling of his family reveals a pope whose personal life and political ambitions were inseparable. His relationship with Marozia allowed him to rise to power but also kept him beholden to the ambitions of her family. His role as a father, while less publicly discussed, had far-reaching consequences, as his son's elevation to the papacy ensured that the Theophylact family's influence continued to shape the Church for years to come. Ultimately, Sergius' familial ties were a defining feature of his papacy, demonstrating the extent to which personal relationships could corrupt and manipulate the highest office in the Church during this dark period of its history.

3. Pope John X (914–928)

Life and Background

Pope John X's rise to the papacy is deeply rooted in the complex web of political and personal relationships that defined early 10th-century Rome, particularly his relationship with **Theodora**, a powerful and influential Roman noblewoman. John X's career and eventual elevation to the papacy were significantly shaped by his connection to Theodora and her family, who, along with her husband, Theophylact of Tusculum, exercised considerable control over the Church during what is often referred to as the "Saeculum Obscurum" or "Dark Age of the Papacy."

John X was born in the late 9th century in the region of Romagna, Italy, and began his clerical career as a bishop, rising through the ecclesiastical ranks with the support of influential Roman families. His talents as a diplomat and church leader earned him favor, but it was his relationship with Theodora that solidified his path to the papal throne. Theodora was one of the most powerful women in Rome, wielding considerable influence over the city's political and religious landscape. Her family, the Theophylacts, effectively controlled Rome during this period, using their power to influence the selection of popes and dominate Church affairs.

It is widely believed that John X's relationship with Theodora was not merely political but also romantic. Contemporary sources, including the **Liber Pontificalis**, suggest that Theodora used her position and personal influence to promote John X to higher offices within the Church. Their relationship was a combination of personal affection and political ambition, with Theodora recognizing John's talents and using her power to ensure his rise.

John X's early career was marked by his appointment as **Archbishop of Ravenna**, a significant position that gave him authority over a key region in Italy. It was during his time as archbishop that his relationship with Theodora deepened. She played a crucial role in promoting his candidacy for the papacy after the death of Pope Lando in 914. With Theodora's backing, John X was elected pope, cementing the Theophylact family's influence over the Church. His election further entrenched the practice of Roman aristocratic families manipulating the papal office for their own political gain, a hallmark of this era of the papacy.

Once in power, John X proved to be an effective and capable pope, particularly in matters of military and diplomatic strategy. He worked to strengthen the Church's position in Italy and Europe, notably organizing a coalition that defeated the **Saracens** at the **Battle of Garigliano** in 915, a significant victory that enhanced his reputation as a political leader. Despite these successes, John X's papacy remained overshadowed by his connection to Theodora and her family. His reliance on the Theophylacts for political support made him vulnerable to the shifting dynamics of Roman politics.

The relationship between John X and Theodora, while instrumental in his rise to power, also contributed to his downfall. After Theodora's death, her daughter, **Marozia**, assumed control of the family's political network and sought to exert her own influence over the papacy. Marozia, who had previously been involved in the scandal surrounding Pope Sergius III, turned against John X, perceiving him as a rival for control over Rome's political landscape. Her animosity toward John X eventually led to his removal from power and imprisonment in 928.

John X's life and background reflect the volatile nature of the papacy during this period, where powerful Roman families wielded immense influence over Church affairs. His relationship with Theodora, while initially beneficial to his career, became a symbol of the deep entanglement between personal relationships and papal politics. Although John X was an effective leader in many respects, his reliance on Theodora and the Theophylact family ultimately undermined his papacy, making him a victim of the very power struggles that had elevated him to the highest office in the Church.

In the end, Pope John X's legacy is defined by both his political achievements and his personal relationships. His connection to Theodora played a critical role in shaping his career, but it also left him vulnerable to the shifting allegiances and ambitions of Rome's noble families. His rise and fall reflect the complex interplay between personal ambition, political power, and spiritual authority that characterized the papacy during one of its most troubled eras.

Scandals and Exploits

POPE JOHN X'S PAPACY is enveloped in scandal, particularly regarding his alleged romantic relationship with **Theodora**, a powerful Roman noblewoman, and accusations that he may have fathered children. These accusations, combined with the volatile political landscape of the time, highlight the complexities of John X's rise to power and the morally compromised environment in which the papacy operated during the early 10th century.

John X's relationship with Theodora was central to his political ascension. Theodora, the wife of Theophylact of Tusculum, was one of the most influential women in Rome, controlling much of the city's political affairs through her family's dominance. Historical sources, particularly the **Liber Pontificalis** and later chroniclers, describe Theodora as having a strong influence over John X's rise to power, with many claiming that their relationship was not purely political, but also romantic.

It was widely believed that Theodora used her intimate connection with John X to promote his career within the Church. She ensured his appointment as **Archbishop of Ravenna**, one of the most prestigious ecclesiastical positions in Italy, before maneuvering him into the papacy in 914. This relationship, while shrouded in secrecy, was an open secret in Rome, with many contemporary writers suggesting that Theodora's influence extended far beyond political support. Some went as far as to accuse John X of fathering children with Theodora, though concrete evidence of this is lacking, and it remains a point of speculation rather than historical certainty.

Despite the lack of solid proof, these rumors about John X fathering children served to undermine his moral authority as pope, as the Church was moving toward stricter enforcement of clerical celibacy. The fact that he was so closely aligned with Theodora, both politically and possibly romantically, was seen as further evidence of the growing corruption and worldly entanglements of the papacy during this period. This alleged relationship painted a picture of a pope who was as much a political figure as a spiritual leader, reliant on personal connections to maintain his power.

Theodora's role in John X's rise to power cannot be overstated. Her influence over the papal selection process was instrumental in securing his election, and it is widely believed that without her backing, John X would not have been elevated to the papal throne. This alliance, however, came with its own set of challenges. By accepting Theodora's patronage, John X tied his fortunes to the Theophylact family, whose grip on Rome's political affairs was absolute. As long as Theodora remained a powerful figure, John X's position was secure, but the inherent scandal of their alleged relationship tainted his reputation, even as he led the Church.

John X's romantic entanglements with Theodora were also part of the broader narrative of moral decline within the papacy during the "Saeculum Obscurum" or "Dark Age of the Papacy." During this era, popes were often seen as more concerned with political power and personal gain than with their spiritual responsibilities. John X's close relationship with Theodora exemplified this trend, as it highlighted the extent to which noble families could manipulate the papal office to advance their own interests.

While his relationship with Theodora helped John X rise to power, it also made him vulnerable to political enemies, particularly after Theodora's death. Following her passing, her daughter **Marozia**, another key player in Roman politics, turned against John X, viewing him as a rival for control over the city and the papacy. Marozia, who had also been involved in papal scandals—most notably with Pope Sergius III—engineered John X's eventual downfall. In 928, she orchestrated his arrest and imprisonment, effectively ending his papacy and leading to his death in captivity.

John X's papacy, while marked by significant political and military achievements, was overshadowed by the personal scandals that surrounded him. His alleged affair with Theodora and the accusations of fathering children added to the perception that the papacy during this period was mired in moral corruption. Although John X was a capable leader in many respects, particularly in his efforts to defend Italy from foreign invasions, the rumors of his personal life and the influence of powerful women like Theodora and Marozia served to undermine his papal authority.

In conclusion, the scandals surrounding Pope John X's relationship with Theodora, including accusations of fathering children, played a significant role in shaping the perception of his papacy. While there is no definitive proof of these claims, they reflect the broader corruption of the Church during this period, where political alliances and personal relationships often took precedence over spiritual leadership. John X's reliance on Theodora's influence, both personal and political, was a double-edged sword, contributing to both his rise and eventual fall.

Corruption

POPE JOHN X'S PAPACY occurred during one of the most infamous and morally compromised periods in Church history, often referred to as the **"Pornocracy"** or the **"Rule of the Harlots."** This era, spanning much of the 10th century, was characterized by the extraordinary influence that powerful Roman noblewomen, such as **Theodora** and her daughter **Marozia**, wielded over the papacy and the broader political landscape of Rome. The "Pornocracy" reflected a time when the papacy was more closely aligned with personal ambitions, corruption, and power struggles than with spiritual guidance, and Pope John X played a central role in this notorious chapter of Church history.

The term "Pornocracy" derives from the overwhelming control that these noblewomen exercised over the papacy. Theodora and Marozia, as matriarchs of the Theophylact family, dominated Roman politics, using their wealth, social standing, and influence to manipulate papal elections and install popes who served their interests. While the term carries pejorative connotations, the reality of the period is that the papacy had fallen under the control of Rome's aristocratic elite, with powerful families, led by these women, vying for dominance over the Church's leadership.

Theodora, a central figure in the "Pornocracy," was closely associated with John X, and it was widely believed that her romantic and political relationship with him played a significant role in his rise to power. Theodora and her husband, **Theophylact of Tusculum**, controlled much of Rome through their military and political connections, and they used this power to influence the election of popes. Theodora's support of John X, whom she allegedly elevated through their personal relationship, cemented the perception that the papacy was no longer an independent spiritual authority but rather a tool of the Roman nobility.

John X's elevation to the papacy in 914 was a direct result of Theodora's influence. Her backing, along with that of her family, ensured his election after the death of Pope Lando. However, while John X was an accomplished politician and military leader, his papacy was overshadowed by his deep connection to Theodora, and later, by the political machinations of Marozia. The very foundation of John X's reign was built on the manipulation of the papal office by these powerful women, a fact that tainted his reputation and placed him squarely within the context of the "Pornocracy."

Although John X did achieve significant military successes—most notably his defeat of the **Saracens** at the **Battle of Garigliano** in 915—his reliance on Theodora's support and the perception of his personal relationship with her left him vulnerable to accusations of corruption. His papacy, while effective in some respects, was seen as an extension of the Theophylact family's power, rather than a genuine spiritual leadership. The intertwining of personal relationships and papal politics during this period led to widespread cynicism about the Church's role and its ability to maintain moral authority.

Marozia, Theodora's daughter, would later come to play a critical role in John X's downfall. After Theodora's death, Marozia assumed control of the Theophylact family's political operations, and like her mother, she sought to control the papacy. Marozia, who had previously been involved with Pope Sergius III and was the mother of **Pope John XI**, viewed John X as both a rival and an obstacle to her own power. Although John X had initially been an ally of the Theophylact family, Marozia's ambitions were boundless, and she eventually orchestrated a coup to remove him from power.

In 928, Marozia led a rebellion against John X, capturing him and imprisoning him in the **Castel Sant'Angelo**. This coup, carried out with the backing of the Roman aristocracy and her family's military resources, effectively ended John X's papacy. He died in captivity, either by murder or under harsh conditions, and Marozia installed her own candidate as pope, further cementing her control over the papal office. Marozia's actions demonstrated the extent to which the papacy had become a political prize to be won, with little regard for its spiritual significance.

The "Pornocracy" era, in which Pope John X was a key player, was a period of unparalleled corruption in the Church's history. The papacy, rather than serving as a moral and spiritual guide for the Christian world, became a pawn in the power struggles of Rome's aristocratic families, particularly the Theophylacts. John X's reliance on Theodora for his rise to power, and his ultimate downfall at the hands of Marozia, highlighted the way in which personal relationships and political ambitions had come to dominate the leadership of the Church.

In analyzing John X's role in the "Pornocracy," it becomes clear that his papacy was shaped more by the political desires of Theodora and Marozia than by his own ecclesiastical vision. His achievements, particularly in military affairs, were significant, but they were overshadowed by the perception that he was a pawn in the hands of powerful women who sought to control Rome. The corruption that defined this period had long-lasting consequences for the Church, leading to a decline in the papacy's moral authority and contributing to the overall instability of the papal office during the 10th century.

Ultimately, Pope John X's involvement in the "Pornocracy" era exemplifies the deep entanglement of the papacy with secular and personal interests. His relationship with Theodora and his reliance on the Theophylact family for power marked him as a participant in the corruption that plagued the Church during this dark period, and his eventual downfall at the hands of Marozia underscores the volatile nature of the papacy during this time.

Handling His Family

POPE JOHN X'S RUMORED relationships, particularly with the powerful Roman noblewoman **Theodora**, and the speculated existence of children born from these relationships, posed unique challenges for him as the leader of the Catholic Church. Navigating the complex demands of the papal office while dealing with the rumors and realities of his personal life would have required a delicate balance, especially during a time when the Church's moral authority was increasingly questioned due to corruption and political intrigue.

While historical records do not provide definitive proof of John X fathering children, his close relationship with Theodora was well-known. Theodora, alongside her husband Theophylact, essentially controlled Rome and the papacy through her influence, and her connection to John X was instrumental in his rise to power. Some sources, particularly the **Liber Pontificalis**, suggest that this relationship was not purely political and that it may have been romantic, with rumors circulating that John X fathered children with Theodora.

If John X did indeed father children during his time in the Church, managing this aspect of his personal life while holding the papal office would have required significant discretion. Given the increasingly stringent expectations surrounding clerical celibacy—though not yet universally enforced—any public acknowledgment of a family would have severely undermined his papal authority. Therefore, it is likely that John X sought to keep any such relationships and offspring hidden from public view, maintaining a veneer of celibacy and piety to avoid scandal.

In terms of navigating these relationships while leading the Church, John X would have relied heavily on his political alliances, particularly with the Theophylact family, to shield him from public scrutiny. The fact that the Theophylacts were essentially the power behind the throne in Rome meant that they had the means to suppress rumors and protect John X's reputation from outright collapse. Theodora herself, as a master of political manipulation, would have likely played a role in managing any fallout from their alleged relationship, using her influence to ensure that any children remained out of the public eye.

However, even with the Theophylacts' protection, the mere suggestion that John X was involved in a romantic relationship and potentially fathered children would have created tension within the Church. His position as pope required him to uphold certain moral standards, and any perceived failure to do so could have weakened his authority, both spiritually and politically. John X's ability to navigate these rumors without completely losing the trust of the Roman clergy and the broader Christian community is a testament to his political acumen.

If John X did have children, there is little evidence to suggest that he openly acknowledged or supported them in a public manner. The culture of secrecy surrounding the papacy at the time, coupled with the political maneuverings of powerful Roman families, meant that any offspring would have likely been kept at a distance from the papal court. It is possible that they were raised quietly under the protection of the Theophylact family, but without public recognition or the privileges that might have come with being the children of a pope.

The scandalous nature of these rumors, however, did little to endear John X to his rivals, particularly after Theodora's death. His relationship with Theodora's daughter, **Marozia**, became increasingly fraught as Marozia sought to control the papacy herself. Marozia, who had her own history of relationships with popes—most notably Pope Sergius III—saw John X as a rival for control over Rome and the Church. If John X had fathered children with Theodora, this would have only added to the tension between him and Marozia, who sought to protect her own political interests and those of her offspring.

Ultimately, John X's downfall came at the hands of Marozia, who orchestrated his arrest and imprisonment in 928. Whether or not his rumored family played a direct role in his political demise is unclear, but his close ties to the Theophylact family undoubtedly contributed to the power struggles that led to his eventual ousting. His ability to manage his personal relationships while serving as pope became increasingly difficult as the political landscape shifted, and he ultimately became a victim of the same power dynamics that had initially propelled him to the papal throne.

In conclusion, Pope John X likely navigated his rumored relationships and potential children through a combination of secrecy, political alliances, and the protection offered by the Theophylact family. While he may have successfully maintained his position for much of his papacy, the personal and political entanglements that defined his rise to power ultimately contributed to his downfall. His papacy serves as a reminder of the delicate balance that popes during this period had to strike between their personal lives and their public roles as spiritual leaders, especially during an era when corruption and scandal plagued the Church.

4. Pope John XII (955–964)

Life and Bacskground

Pope John XII, born **Octavianus**, was one of the youngest and most controversial figures to ever ascend to the papal throne. Born around 937 into the powerful **Crescentii family**, which controlled much of Rome during the 10th century, Octavianus was thrust into a position of immense influence from an early age. His father, **Alberic II of Spoleto**, a Roman noble and ruler of the city, groomed his son for both secular and spiritual leadership. In an unprecedented move, Alberic ensured that his son would inherit not only his earthly power but also the spiritual leadership of the Catholic Church. As a result, Octavianus was elected pope in December 955 at the astonishingly young age of 18, taking the name **John XII**.

The appointment of someone so young to the papacy was highly unusual and was largely a result of the Crescentii family's dominance over Roman politics at the time. His election highlighted the extent to which the papal office had become deeply intertwined with the power struggles of Rome's noble families. The papacy during this period was as much a political office as it was a spiritual one, and the appointment of John XII was seen by many as a way for the Crescentii family to consolidate their control over both the Church and the city of Rome.

John XII's papacy quickly gained a notorious reputation, largely due to his scandalous personal life. Almost immediately after his election, rumors began to circulate about his immoral behavior, which included allegations of debauchery, violence, and rampant sexual misconduct. Unlike other popes of his era who at least attempted to maintain a facade of piety, John XII's actions were brazen and openly defied the moral expectations of the papal office.

Contemporary sources, particularly from **Liudprand of Cremona**, paint a damning picture of John XII. He is described as indulging in a life of excess and sin, including hosting lavish parties, gambling, and engaging in open sexual relationships with women. These included not only noblewomen but also widows, nuns, and even his own female relatives. His reign became synonymous with vice, and his papal palace was rumored to have been transformed into what many referred to as a "brothel," a stark contrast to the sanctity the office was supposed to represent.

John XII's behavior was shocking even for an era that was no stranger to scandal. He was accused of committing multiple sins, including adultery, incest, and the ordination of priests for money. His papacy embodied the moral decline of the Church during the **Saeculum Obscurum** or "The Dark Age of the Papacy," a time when the papal office was frequently under the control of corrupt Roman aristocratic families and became a pawn in their political games.

Despite his moral failings, John XII continued to wield considerable political power. His papacy was marked by ongoing conflicts with rival factions within Rome and with the Holy Roman Emperor, Otto I. In an attempt to maintain his grip on power, John XII sought alliances with various Italian nobles, but his unstable leadership and personal indulgences made it difficult for him to effectively govern. His erratic behavior ultimately alienated many of his allies, and he became increasingly isolated as his reign progressed.

In 963, his poor political judgment led him to a conflict with Otto I, who had initially been one of John's strongest supporters. John betrayed Otto by conspiring with his enemies, leading to his deposition by a council called by Otto. John XII fled Rome and was replaced by **Leo VIII**, though he briefly regained the papal throne before his untimely death in 964. He died under mysterious circumstances, with some accounts claiming he was killed by a jealous husband during an adulterous affair, while others suggest he died of a stroke.

John XII's papacy remains one of the most infamous in the history of the Catholic Church. His youth, combined with his scandalous personal life and erratic behavior, made him a symbol of the moral decay that plagued the Church during this period. Despite his brief tenure, his reign serves as a stark reminder of the challenges the Church faced in balancing spiritual leadership with the intense political pressures of the time.

Scandals and Exploits

POPE JOHN XII'S PAPACY was one of the most scandalous and notorious in the history of the Catholic Church, marked by widespread accusations of immorality, corruption, and sexual debauchery. His personal life and conduct were so outrageous that his tenure as pope is often cited as one of the lowest points in the history of the papacy. Among the many allegations against him were claims of **orgies**, rampant sexual misconduct, and even **multiple mistresses and illegitimate children**.

John XII became pope at the age of 18, and rather than embracing the spiritual and moral responsibilities of the office, he turned the **Lateran Palace**—the official residence of the pope—into a notorious center of vice and excess. According to contemporary sources, most notably **Liudprand of Cremona**, a diplomat and chronicler, John XII transformed the papal residence into what was referred to as a "brothel." The pope was accused of hosting wild parties and **orgies** within the very walls of the Vatican, bringing disrepute to an office that was meant to embody piety and moral leadership.

Orgies in the Lateran Palace: The accusations against John XII included holding extravagant feasts that devolved into orgies. It was said that he invited noblewomen, widows, and even nuns to participate in these licentious gatherings, completely disregarding the sacredness of his position. According to Liudprand of Cremona, "he turned the Lateran Palace into a den of iniquity," with reports of debauchery and open sexual relationships being commonplace. The Lateran, which should have been the spiritual heart of the Church, became a symbol of corruption and decadence during his papacy.

Mistresses and Illegitimate Children: John XII was accused of having **numerous mistresses**, many of whom were members of the Roman nobility. These women were drawn to the pope either for his power or due to his family's aristocratic connections. John's behavior scandalized even his contemporaries, as he allegedly showed little regard for clerical celibacy or moral restraint. Among his mistresses, there were rumors of **incestuous relationships** involving close female relatives, which added another layer of controversy to his papacy.

The pope's sexual liaisons were not limited to the nobility. He was also accused of engaging in relationships with **widows, nuns,** and even **his own female relatives**, as well as with women who sought favors or influence within the Church. These illicit relationships, some claimed, resulted in **multiple illegitimate children**, although the exact number or identity of these offspring remains uncertain. His failure to observe any semblance of clerical celibacy made him a stark contrast to the idealized image of the pope as a moral and spiritual leader.

Incest and Blasphemy: In addition to accusations of adultery and fornication, some of the charges against John XII were even more scandalous. He was rumored to have engaged in **incest** with his own nieces, further shocking an already scandalized Church. These accusations painted a picture of a man who had little respect for the sanctity of family, let alone the expectations of moral purity that his office demanded.

On top of his sexual improprieties, John XII was also accused of **blasphemy and sacrilege**. Some accounts claim that he toasted to pagan gods during his drinking parties, which, if true, would have been an incredible affront to Christian doctrine. This, combined with his alleged desecration of the papal office, led many to see his papacy as emblematic of the Church's moral decay during the **Saeculum Obscurum** or "Dark Age of the Papacy."

Ordinations for Money and Simony: Apart from his sexual scandals, John XII was accused of engaging in **simony**, the practice of selling Church offices and sacraments. It was said that he frequently accepted bribes in exchange for ordinations, which undermined the integrity of the Church's hierarchy. This practice of selling ecclesiastical positions to the highest bidder not only corrupted the Church but also alienated those who expected moral leadership from the pope.

Political Exploits and Betrayals: John XII's papacy was also marked by political miscalculations and betrayals. One of his most significant political blunders was his betrayal of **Otto I**, the Holy Roman Emperor. Initially, John XII had sought Otto's support to consolidate his position in Italy and secure the papal states, and in return, Otto I was crowned emperor in 962. However, soon after, John XII conspired with Otto's enemies, seeking to oust the emperor from power and regain full control of Rome. This betrayal led to Otto's invasion of Rome and the eventual deposition of John XII in 963.

Otto I convened a council of bishops and clergy in Rome, which levied multiple charges against John XII. The accusations included **adultery, incest, perjury, blasphemy**, and **murder**—all of which painted the pope as a man wholly unfit for the office. The council declared him deposed and replaced him with **Leo VIII**, though John XII briefly reclaimed the papal throne before his sudden death in 964.

Mysterious Death: John XII's death, much like his life, was shrouded in scandal. He died under suspicious circumstances at the age of 27. While some sources claim that he died of a stroke, others allege that he was killed by a jealous husband who caught him in bed with his wife. This latter version of his death only adds to the sensational and scandalous legacy of his papacy.

In conclusion, Pope John XII's reign was one of the most scandal-ridden in papal history. His flagrant disregard for the moral and spiritual responsibilities of the papacy, coupled with his involvement in sexual debauchery, corruption, and political betrayals, made his tenure as pope a symbol of the Church's profound moral decline during the 10th century. His papacy remains infamous for its excesses, and John XII's life serves as a stark reminder of how deeply entangled the papal office had become with the vices and corruptions of Roman nobility.

Corruption

POPE JOHN XII'S PAPACY is widely regarded as one of the most corrupt and scandalous in the history of the Catholic Church. His reign was filled with allegations of immorality, criminal behavior, and the blatant misuse of papal power, making his tenure one of the most infamous in the long history of the papacy. Coming to power at the tender age of 18, John XII quickly became a symbol of the moral decay that had gripped the papacy during the **Saeculum Obscurum**, or **"Dark Age of the Papacy"**, a period notorious for political manipulation, corruption, and the dominance of Roman aristocratic families over the Church.

John XII's papacy was marked by a near-complete disregard for the moral responsibilities associated with the papal office. From the beginning, he used his position not for the spiritual betterment of the Church but for his own personal pleasure and gain. His abuse of power was characterized by three major forms of corruption: **sexual immorality**, **criminal acts**, and **political treachery**.

Sexual Immorality: One of the defining characteristics of John XII's papacy was the widespread rumors and accusations of **sexual debauchery**. Contemporary chroniclers, most notably **Liudprand of Cremona**, accused John XII of turning the **Lateran Palace** into what was effectively a den of vice. His reign was rife with allegations of engaging in **orgies**, maintaining multiple **mistresses**, and fathering **illegitimate children**. There were even accusations of **incest**, with rumors that John XII had sexual relations with his own female relatives. His sexual exploits were notorious throughout Rome, and he flaunted his disregard for clerical celibacy and moral conduct openly, bringing deep shame and scandal to the papal office.

Liudprand of Cremona's accounts, though written with a critical eye, describe John XII's Lateran Palace as a site of continuous feasting, gambling, and licentious behavior, where women—noble and common—were treated as objects of the pope's desire. His open indulgence in sexual misconduct was unprecedented for a man occupying the papal throne, causing outrage among clergy and nobility alike.

Simony and Ecclesiastical Corruption: In addition to his sexual misconduct, John XII was widely accused of **simony**, the selling of Church offices and sacred privileges for money. Simony, a grave sin in the eyes of the Church, undermined the integrity of the ecclesiastical hierarchy and allowed unqualified individuals to gain positions of power simply by paying bribes. John XII allegedly took bribes in exchange for ordinations and consecrations, selling bishoprics and priestly positions to the highest bidders, regardless of their spiritual qualifications or dedication to the Church. This practice not only degraded the sanctity of the Church but also allowed corruption to seep into all levels of its administration.

Political Corruption and Betrayal: John XII's reign was further marred by his political incompetence and betrayal of his allies. The most significant example of his political treachery was his relationship with **Holy Roman Emperor Otto I**. Initially, John XII sought the protection of Otto I to secure his position as pope and maintain control over the papal states. In 962, John crowned Otto as the **Holy Roman Emperor**, thereby strengthening his alliance with the most powerful ruler in Europe. However, almost immediately after solidifying this alliance, John began plotting against Otto, conspiring with Otto's enemies in Italy to overthrow the emperor's influence over Rome.

This act of betrayal, motivated by John's desire to maintain absolute control over Rome and the papal territories, led to severe consequences. Otto, angered by John XII's treachery, marched on Rome and convened a council in 963 to address the numerous allegations against the pope. The council, attended by bishops and clergy, accused John XII of **perjury, murder, incest, adultery**, and **simony**. The list of charges was staggering and painted a picture of a pope who had not only abandoned his spiritual duties but had become an outright criminal.

Criminal Acts: Among the charges levied against John XII were serious accusations of **criminal behavior**, including **murder** and **blasphemy**. According to contemporary accounts, John XII was accused of blinding a cardinal, castrating a deacon who later died from his injuries, and even toasting to pagan gods during his drinking bouts. These acts, if true, demonstrated not only his disregard for human life but also a profound disrespect for the sacred office he held. His violent and blasphemous actions further alienated him from the clergy and the broader Christian community.

The council convened by Otto I deposed John XII in December 963 and replaced him with **Leo VIII**, a move that symbolized Otto's attempt to restore moral order to the papacy. However, John XII refused to relinquish his claim to the papal throne and, after Otto left Rome, he rallied his supporters and briefly regained control of the city. His chaotic and corrupt reign came to an abrupt end when he died in May 964, under suspicious circumstances. Some accounts suggest that he was killed by a jealous husband who caught him in bed with his wife, while others claim that he suffered a fatal stroke.

The Legacy of John XII's Corruption: John XII's reign is often cited as one of the darkest periods in the history of the papacy. His actions contributed to the broader decline of the Church's moral authority during the **10th century** and underscored the vulnerability of the papal office to manipulation by Roman aristocratic families. The fact that such a young and inexperienced individual could ascend to the papacy through the influence of his family speaks to the extent of corruption that permeated the Church during this era. His reign became a symbol of how far the papacy had fallen, and his name is often invoked as a cautionary tale of the dangers of unchecked power and moral decay within the Church.

In conclusion, Pope John XII's papacy stands out as one of the most corrupt and scandalous in the annals of the Catholic Church. His open indulgence in sexual immorality, simony, and violent acts, combined with his betrayal of allies and political incompetence, left a lasting stain on the reputation of the papal office. His reign exemplified the low point of the papacy during the "Dark Age of the Papacy," a time when spiritual leadership was often overshadowed by corruption and worldly ambition.

Handling His Family

POPE JOHN XII'S PAPACY was marked by chaos, scandal, and a lack of moral restraint, and his personal relationships were no exception. Throughout his reign, he exhibited little concern for the moral responsibilities associated with the papal office, and it is evident that he struggled—or outright neglected—to manage his personal relationships in any meaningful way. Given the numerous accusations of sexual misconduct, including relationships with **multiple mistresses, noblewomen, nuns**, and even alleged **incestuous affairs**, it seems clear that John XII was more interested in indulging his desires than maintaining any semblance of familial or relational responsibility.

Despite the allegations that he fathered **illegitimate children**, historical records provide little information about how, or even if, John XII acknowledged or supported these offspring. The accounts of his papacy paint a picture of a man who was primarily concerned with the pursuit of pleasure, wealth, and power, often at the expense of his spiritual and moral duties. It is likely that any children he may have fathered were either ignored or kept hidden to avoid further scandal—although, given the openness with which John conducted his immoral activities, it is possible that he made little effort to conceal these relationships or the resulting children.

John XII's handling of his personal relationships, particularly his rumored **incestuous liaisons** and **mistresses**, appeared to be dictated by self-interest and power rather than affection or familial loyalty. Unlike other popes who may have faced similar scandals but sought to protect their family from public scrutiny, John XII seemed largely indifferent to the consequences of his actions. His mistresses were reportedly drawn from both the nobility and the clergy, and he is alleged to have used his papal authority to seduce women and exploit his power for personal gratification.

Given the accusations of **incest**—some sources suggest relationships with **nieces** or other close female relatives—it is clear that John XII's reign was not only morally compromised but also deeply rooted in the decadence of Rome's aristocratic families. These relationships, if true, would have further alienated him from his role as a spiritual leader and contributed to his downfall, as the Church's moral authority was rapidly eroding under his leadership.

It is important to consider the political and familial context in which John XII operated. As a member of the powerful **Crescentii family**, his early rise to power was largely orchestrated by his father, **Alberic II of Spoleto**, who sought to secure both secular and spiritual dominance in Rome by installing his teenage son as pope. John XII's family wielded immense political influence, but it is clear that he used his papal position for personal gain rather than familial responsibility. Despite the power of the Crescentii family, John XII's personal indulgences and disregard for his public role strained these relationships, contributing to the overall instability of his reign.

As for how John XII balanced these personal entanglements with his papal duties, it seems that his chaotic lifestyle left little room for the structured governance expected of a pope. He was frequently accused of neglecting his spiritual responsibilities, and it is likely that his personal relationships were managed with the same level of indifference. Rather than fostering alliances or securing legitimate heirs to carry on his family's legacy, John XII appears to have treated his relationships as temporary and transactional, focused more on pleasure than on long-term familial bonds.

Additionally, John XII's disregard for the Church's moral standards meant that he did not see the need to manage or conceal his relationships, leading to widespread criticism and allegations that tarnished his reputation. His inability—or unwillingness—to handle these relationships responsibly only compounded the scandals that plagued his papacy, as his enemies used these personal failings to depose him and ultimately end his chaotic reign.

In conclusion, Pope John XII's management of his personal relationships was as morally dubious as the rest of his papacy. His reign, filled with accusations of sexual misconduct, incest, and illegitimate children, demonstrates his disregard for both the Church's teachings and the familial duties he might have been expected to fulfill. His relationships were driven by power and pleasure, with little evidence of meaningful commitment or responsibility toward the individuals involved, further contributing to his legacy as one of the most corrupt and scandalous popes in history.

5. Pope Benedict IX (1032–1048)

Life and Background

Pope Benedict IX is remembered as one of the most controversial and morally compromised figures in the history of the papacy. Born **Theophylactus of Tusculum** around 1012 into the powerful **Tusculani** family, he became pope at an extraordinarily young age. His election to the papacy in 1032 is often regarded as a product of the deeply entrenched political manipulation by Roman noble families, particularly the Tusculani, who wielded significant influence over both secular and ecclesiastical affairs in Rome.

Benedict IX was the nephew of two previous popes, **Benedict VIII** and **John XIX**, both of whom had also come to power through the influence of the Tusculani family. His father, **Alberic III, Count of Tusculum**, was a prominent figure in Roman politics and had orchestrated Benedict's rise to the papacy. At the time of his election, Benedict IX was believed to be only about **20 years old**, making him one of the youngest popes in history. His youth and inexperience, combined with the corrupt manner in which he attained the papacy, set the stage for one of the most scandal-ridden papacies in the medieval Church.

The Tusculani family controlled much of the political landscape of Rome, and their influence over the papal office was part of a broader trend during this period, where powerful aristocratic families used the papacy as a tool to consolidate their political power. Benedict IX's election was no exception; his appointment was secured through the wealth and connections of his family rather than any demonstration of spiritual or theological aptitude. His early life had been one of privilege, shaped by the luxuries and intrigues of the Roman nobility rather than the religious devotion expected of a future pope.

As a result, Benedict IX's papacy was marked from the start by an overwhelming sense of impropriety. Contemporary sources, particularly those written by **St. Peter Damian** and **Cardinal Bonizo of Sutri**, describe Benedict IX as corrupt, immoral, and utterly unfit for the papal office. He was accused of leading a scandalous personal life, indulging in worldly pleasures, and showing little concern for the spiritual responsibilities of the papacy. These early accusations foreshadowed what would become one of the most tumultuous and controversial periods in papal history.

Despite the fact that Benedict IX held the highest office in the Christian world, he was more interested in the power, wealth, and luxuries that came with the title than in leading the Church. His reign was characterized by rampant corruption, simony (the selling of church offices), and scandalous behavior, which ultimately led to a series of crises that destabilized both the papacy and Rome. Benedict's disregard for the moral expectations of his role caused widespread disillusionment among the clergy and laity alike, leading to growing calls for his removal.

Benedict IX's papacy is particularly notorious for its instability, as he held the papal office **three separate times** between 1032 and 1048. His reign was interrupted by multiple abdications and depositions, as both external political pressures and his own personal failings led to periods of exile and disgrace. His first papacy ended in 1044 when he was forced to flee Rome in the face of a popular uprising against his corrupt and immoral behavior. His departure from the city allowed for the election of an antipope, **Sylvester III**, but Benedict would return shortly afterward to reclaim his position, plunging the papacy into chaos.

One of the most notorious episodes in Benedict IX's papacy came in **1045**, when he **sold the papal office** to his godfather, **John Gratian**, who became **Pope Gregory VI**. This act of simony, unprecedented in the history of the Church, further cemented Benedict IX's legacy as a deeply corrupt and unworthy pontiff. Benedict's decision to sell the papacy was motivated by his desire to marry, though the marriage never took place. Despite abdicating, Benedict would later attempt to regain the papal throne, leading to further instability and conflict within the Church.

In total, Benedict IX's tumultuous career as pope spanned three terms: from 1032 to 1044, again from 1045 to 1046, and briefly in 1047–1048. His repeated returns to power underscored the degree to which the papacy had become a tool of personal ambition and family politics, rather than a sacred institution dedicated to spiritual leadership.

Benedict IX's life and background as a young, inexperienced pope thrust into power by a corrupt aristocratic family epitomize the broader issues facing the papacy during the **11th century**. His papacy contributed to the growing calls for reform within the Church, which would eventually lead to the **Gregorian Reforms** aimed at curbing simony, enforcing clerical celibacy, and restoring moral integrity to the papal office.

In conclusion, Pope Benedict IX's rise to power was a direct result of the Tusculani family's dominance over Roman politics and their ability to manipulate the papal office for their own ends. His youth, inexperience, and scandalous behavior made him one of the most infamous popes in history, and his repeated abdications, depositions, and corrupt dealings deeply damaged the reputation of the papacy during one of its darkest periods.

Scandals and Exploits

POPE BENEDICT IX'S papacy is infamous for its scandalous nature, marked by a life of moral depravity, sexual misconduct, and unprecedented corruption. His reign is widely regarded as one of the lowest points in the history of the papacy, with Benedict IX indulging in excesses that shocked even his contemporaries. Among the many scandals attributed to him were **numerous sexual indiscretions, allegations of homosexuality**, and the **sale of the papacy**—an act of corruption that has no parallel in Church history.

Sexual Scandals: Benedict IX's personal life was rife with accusations of immorality, and his papacy became synonymous with sexual licentiousness. Contemporary sources describe him as leading a lifestyle filled with indulgence, vice, and debauchery. Chroniclers such as **St. Peter Damian** and **Cardinal Bonizo of Sutri** wrote of Benedict's affairs with women, men, and even accusations of **rape**, presenting him as a figure completely unrestrained by the moral and spiritual responsibilities of the papacy.

St. Peter Damian, a reformer and an outspoken critic of clerical corruption, described Benedict IX as being "a disgrace to the Chair of St. Peter" due to his lustful and scandalous behavior. He was accused of hosting orgies in the **Lateran Palace**, turning what should have been a sacred space into a site of sexual excess. His lifestyle was seen as a direct affront to the expectations of the Church, particularly at a time when the papacy was supposed to embody spiritual purity and moral guidance.

Allegations of Homosexuality: In addition to his relationships with women, Benedict IX faced allegations of **homosexual behavior**, which, in the deeply conservative and religious climate of medieval Europe, was considered a grave sin. While the details of these accusations remain vague, sources suggest that Benedict was involved in relationships with both men and women, further contributing to the perception that he had completely abandoned any semblance of clerical celibacy or moral restraint.

His sexual exploits, both heterosexual and homosexual, became a source of public scandal and outrage, especially among reformers who sought to restore the moral integrity of the Church. Benedict's flagrant disregard for clerical celibacy was emblematic of the broader issues of corruption that plagued the Church during this period, leading to widespread calls for reform.

Sale of the Papacy: One of the most notorious acts of Benedict IX's papacy, and a singular moment of corruption in the history of the Church, was his decision to **sell the papal office**. In **1045**, after years of scandal and public discontent, Benedict IX decided to abdicate the papal throne. The reasons for his abdication were highly irregular—Benedict allegedly sought to marry a woman, which required him to step down from the papacy.

Rather than simply renouncing his position, Benedict sold the papal office to his godfather, **John Gratian**, for a large sum of money. John Gratian, a respected priest, became **Pope Gregory VI** after purchasing the papacy. This act of **simony** (the selling of Church offices), while not uncommon at lower levels of the Church, was unprecedented at the highest level of ecclesiastical power. Benedict's decision to sell the papacy was a clear indication of how deeply corruption had seeped into the Church, with the papal throne being treated as a commodity rather than a sacred office.

The sale of the papacy further destabilized the Church, as it called into question the legitimacy of the papal office itself. While Gregory VI was widely regarded as a more moral figure, the very fact that he had purchased the papacy from Benedict IX tainted his reign and fueled calls for a complete overhaul of the Church's leadership.

Multiple Abdications and Reclamations of the Papacy: Benedict IX's sale of the papacy did not mark the end of his involvement with the Church. After abdicating in 1045, he attempted to reclaim the papal throne several times. In 1047, with the support of the Tusculani family, Benedict returned to Rome and reasserted his claim to the papacy, forcing Gregory VI into exile. However, his second reign was short-lived, as he was deposed once again by **Emperor Henry III** in 1048, who installed **Pope Clement II** in his place.

Benedict's repeated attempts to regain the papacy—motivated by both political ambition and financial greed—further destabilized the Church and contributed to the perception of the papacy as a corrupt institution. His chaotic reign saw multiple claimants to the papal throne, as rival factions vied for control of Rome and the Church.

Legacy of Scandal and Reform: Benedict IX's papacy is remembered as one of the most scandalous in the history of the Catholic Church. His indulgence in sexual immorality, his blatant disregard for the spiritual responsibilities of the papal office, and his sale of the papacy all contributed to a period of deep moral crisis within the Church. His actions were seen as emblematic of the broader corruption that plagued the papacy during the 11th century, leading to growing demands for reform.

The repeated scandals of Benedict IX's reign helped galvanize the **Gregorian Reform movement**, which sought to address the issues of simony, clerical celibacy, and the moral integrity of the Church. Reformers like **St. Peter Damian** and later **Pope Gregory VII** drew upon the failures of Benedict IX's papacy as a rallying cry for change, leading to a renewed effort to restore the moral authority of the papacy and prevent further corruption.

In conclusion, Pope Benedict IX's papacy was marked by a series of scandals and moral failures that made him one of the most infamous figures in the history of the Church. His notorious lifestyle, which included sexual scandals, allegations of homosexuality, and the unprecedented sale of the papal office, left a lasting stain on the reputation of the papacy and contributed to the eventual push for reform within the Church. His reign is often cited as one of the darkest periods in papal history, serving as a reminder of the dangers of unchecked power and moral corruption.

Corruption

POPE BENEDICT IX'S papacy stands as a notorious example of the profound corruption that plagued the Catholic Church during the 11th century. His reign was marked by numerous acts of **simony**, the buying and selling of ecclesiastical positions, culminating in the unprecedented sale of the **papal office itself**. Benedict IX's tenure is often cited as a critical factor in the Church's moral decline during this period, symbolizing the extent to which the papacy had become entangled with secular power, personal ambition, and financial gain.

Simony and Ecclesiastical Corruption: Simony, the act of buying or selling Church offices or sacraments, was a widespread issue in the medieval Church, but it reached its most scandalous peak under Benedict IX. Throughout his papacy, Benedict was accused of using his power to sell bishoprics, priesthoods, and other Church positions to the highest bidder, regardless of the spiritual qualifications of the candidates. This practice severely undermined the integrity of the Church, as ecclesiastical positions were awarded based on wealth and influence rather than merit or religious devotion.

The extent of simony during Benedict IX's reign reflected the broader issue of corruption within the Church, where positions of power were seen as commodities to be bought and sold. This blatant disregard for spiritual values contributed to a deepening crisis within the Church, as unqualified and often morally compromised individuals were placed in positions of authority, further eroding the Church's moral standing. Benedict IX's actions fueled widespread disillusionment among both the clergy and the laity, leading to growing calls for reform.

Sale of the Papacy: The most egregious example of Benedict IX's corruption was his **sale of the papal office**. In **1045**, after years of scandal and public outrage over his immoral behavior, Benedict made the unprecedented decision to **sell the papacy** to his godfather, **John**

Gratian, who became **Pope Gregory VI**. This act of simony was not only a personal failure but a watershed moment of corruption for the entire Church. Benedict's sale of the papacy signaled that the highest spiritual office in Christendom could be treated as a mere commodity, subject to the whims of personal ambition and financial transactions.

The circumstances surrounding this sale were unusual. Benedict, still a young man, allegedly wished to marry a woman and saw abdicating the papacy as the only way to fulfill this personal desire. Rather than simply resigning, he chose to sell the position for a substantial sum of money, an act that shocked the Christian world. John Gratian, a pious and well-respected cleric, paid for the papal office with the intention of reforming the Church, but the very nature of his ascent to the papacy—through a financial transaction—cast a shadow over his legitimacy.

Consequences of Selling the Papacy: The sale of the papacy created immediate political and ecclesiastical turmoil. Benedict IX's decision to abdicate and then attempt to reclaim the papal throne multiple times in the following years added to the chaos. In 1047, with the backing of his powerful Tusculani family, Benedict returned to Rome and briefly retook the papacy, leading to a period of confusion where multiple claimants, including Benedict and Gregory VI, vied for control of the Church.

This instability, caused by Benedict's greed and ambition, had severe consequences for the Church's reputation. The notion that the papal office, the spiritual leadership of the entire Christian world, could be bought and sold like a piece of property led to widespread cynicism and anger. Clergy and laity alike began to question the integrity of the Church's leadership, and Benedict's actions contributed to a growing sense that the papacy had become hopelessly corrupt.

The sale of the papacy also intensified calls for reform, both within the Church and from secular rulers. **Holy Roman Emperor Henry III** eventually intervened in 1046, convening the **Council of Sutri** to address the papal crisis. The council deposed both Benedict IX and Gregory VI, as well as **Sylvester III**, another claimant to the papal throne, and installed **Clement II** as pope. Benedict IX's multiple attempts to regain the papacy, combined with the corrupt nature of his reign, had effectively discredited him and deepened the Church's moral and spiritual crisis.

Benedict IX's Contribution to the Church's Moral Decline: Benedict IX's papacy is often regarded as one of the darkest periods in the history of the Catholic Church. His repeated acts of simony, immoral behavior, and willingness to sell the papal office contributed significantly to the moral decline of the Church. By treating the papacy as a personal possession to be bought, sold, and reclaimed at will, Benedict undermined the spiritual authority of the Church and damaged its credibility among Christians across Europe.

His reign exacerbated the widespread perception that the papacy had become corrupted by secular interests and personal greed, an issue that had been building for decades but reached its apex during Benedict's time. The moral decline associated with his papacy helped spark the **Gregorian Reform Movement**, which sought to address the corruption that had taken root in the Church, particularly regarding simony and the need for clerical celibacy.

Reformers like **Pope Gregory VII** would later draw on the lessons of Benedict IX's reign to push for a more spiritually focused and morally rigorous papacy. Benedict's legacy, though negative, served as a critical turning point in the history of the Church, highlighting the urgent need for reform and the restoration of the papacy's spiritual authority.

In conclusion, Pope Benedict IX's papacy was marked by rampant corruption, particularly through acts of simony and his unprecedented sale of the papal office. His morally compromised leadership contributed to the overall decline of the Church's moral standing and created a crisis of legitimacy that would take years to repair. His reign, filled with scandal and immorality, serves as a stark reminder of the dangers of allowing secular and personal interests to dominate the leadership of the Church, ultimately catalyzing the reform efforts that followed.

Handling His Family

POPE BENEDICT IX'S relationships and the possibility of him fathering children have long been the subject of speculation, though the details remain murky. His scandalous lifestyle, marked by numerous sexual indiscretions, led to widespread rumors and accusations of relationships with both men and women. While specific evidence of Benedict IX having children is scarce, it is reasonable to assume that given his notorious behavior, the possibility of illegitimate offspring cannot be ruled out. However, handling his family, particularly if he had children, would have posed significant challenges during his papacy.

Sexual Scandals and Possible Children: Contemporary sources, including the writings of **St. Peter Damian** and **Cardinal Bonizo of Sutri**, frequently criticized Benedict IX for his sexual misconduct. He was known to have maintained relationships with women during his papacy, which was particularly scandalous given the Church's emphasis on clerical celibacy. While there are no definitive records that confirm the existence of his children, his reputation for debauchery and alleged affairs with noblewomen and others suggest the possibility of illegitimate offspring.

If Benedict IX did father children, it is likely that they would have been kept hidden to avoid further scandal, especially as his reign was already fraught with accusations of moral depravity. The Church during this period was rife with corruption, and it would not have been entirely uncommon for popes or other high-ranking clergy to have illegitimate children. However, openly acknowledging such offspring would have further damaged Benedict IX's reputation and the already fragile moral standing of the papacy.

Managing Relationships and Family Ties: Throughout his tumultuous papacy, Benedict IX's relationships with both his family and potential offspring would have been shaped by the power dynamics of the time. As a member of the influential **Tusculani family**, Benedict was primarily focused on maintaining political control over Rome and the papacy. His family had engineered his rise to power, and they likely continued to support him despite the scandals that marred his reign. However, any illegitimate children, if they existed, would have been a source of embarrassment for both Benedict and the Tusculani family, who were deeply involved in the political and religious power struggles of the era.

It is plausible that Benedict's family would have taken steps to conceal or quietly care for any children he may have fathered, keeping them out of public view to avoid further tarnishing his already infamous reputation. The Tusculani family had a vested interest in protecting their political legacy and maintaining control over the papacy, and they likely would have used their influence to manage any potential fallout from Benedict's personal life.

Marriage and Abdication: One of the most notorious moments of Benedict IX's papacy occurred in **1045**, when he sold the papacy to his godfather, **John Gratian**, later Pope Gregory VI. Benedict allegedly abdicated the papacy in order to marry a woman, although the marriage never materialized. This episode suggests that Benedict may have been genuinely interested in pursuing a family life outside of the Church, but his decision to sell the papacy for personal reasons caused outrage and further damaged the Church's moral authority.

While Benedict's attempt to marry might indicate a desire to establish a legitimate family, the failure of the marriage and his subsequent attempts to reclaim the papacy suggest that his personal relationships were driven by self-interest and ambition rather than any genuine desire for stability or family life. His chaotic and morally dubious reign left little room for managing meaningful personal relationships, and any children he may have fathered were likely left to be cared for by others within the Tusculani family.

Implications for the Papacy and Legacy: The potential existence of illegitimate children, combined with Benedict IX's notorious sexual exploits, further eroded the credibility of the papacy during his reign. His failure to adhere to the standards of clerical celibacy and his blatant disregard for the moral responsibilities of his office contributed to the widespread perception that the Church had fallen into moral decay. His relationships and possible children, though speculative, would have added another layer of scandal to an already infamous papacy.

In conclusion, while the details of Pope Benedict IX's personal relationships and possible children remain murky, the implications of his behavior were clear: his reign contributed to the moral decline of the Church, and any illegitimate offspring would have only added to the scandals surrounding his papacy. Benedict IX's handling of his family, if he had children, would likely have been shaped by the need to conceal or quietly manage these relationships to protect the already fragile reputation of the papacy. His chaotic and self-serving approach to both his personal life and his role as pope ultimately solidified his legacy as one of the most corrupt figures in the history of the papacy.

6. Pope Clement IV (1265–1268)

Life and Background

Pope Clement IV, born **Guido le Gros**, had a remarkable and atypical path to the papacy, one that set him apart from many of his predecessors. Born around 1190 in Saint-Gilles-du-Gard, near Nîmes in the south of France, Guido's early life was defined by his role as a **husband, father,** and **layman**—a life vastly different from the traditional clerical route taken by most future popes. His story highlights the unusual circumstances that eventually led him from the secular world to the papal throne.

Before entering the Church, Guido lived as a **nobleman** and a **lawyer**. He came from a well-established family and received a comprehensive education, particularly in law, which prepared him for a career in public service. His background in legal affairs made him a valuable asset to several high-ranking officials in both secular and ecclesiastical settings. As a young man, Guido pursued a successful career as a lawyer in both his native France and in Italy, serving at various courts. During this time, he was deeply immersed in the political and legal matters of the day, gaining the skills that would later serve him well as a Church leader.

Guido's personal life before his ordination was notable because he was **married** and had **children**, a significant departure from the lives of most future popes. He married a noblewoman whose name is not recorded in most historical sources, but it is known that their union produced **two daughters**. He lived with his wife and children, leading a comfortable and respectable life as a family man. His daughters would go on to become nuns, dedicating their lives to religious service—likely a reflection of Guido's deepening faith as he grew older.

Tragedy struck when Guido's wife passed away, leaving him a widower. It was only after her death that Guido began considering a life dedicated to the Church. His transition from family life to religious life is a testament to the profound personal transformation he underwent after the loss of his wife. After his wife's death, Guido gradually withdrew from his secular responsibilities and turned toward a more spiritual path. By all accounts, he was a man of strong personal conviction and piety, which, combined with his legal acumen, made him an appealing candidate for the Church.

Clerical Career: After his wife's death, Guido took the remarkable step of **entering the priesthood**, leaving behind his legal career and noble status. He was ordained as a priest relatively late in life, around the age of 50, a rarity for future popes, most of whom spent their early years in monastic or clerical orders. Despite his late start, Guido's experience as a lawyer and his reputation for wisdom and integrity quickly propelled him through the ranks of the Church.

Guido was appointed **bishop of Le Puy** in 1257 and then **archbishop of Narbonne** shortly afterward. His administrative and diplomatic skills earned him a reputation as a capable and level-headed leader, traits that would become vital during his papacy. He became a trusted advisor to the **French king, Louis IX**, and played a crucial role in mediating political disputes between France and the papal states. His ties to the French crown would continue to influence his papacy, as he often worked to maintain strong relations between France and the Church.

In 1261, Pope Urban IV elevated Guido to the rank of **cardinal**, where his talents were further recognized in Rome. His legal expertise and diplomatic abilities were highly valued by the papacy, and he was entrusted with several important missions, including diplomatic negotiations and matters of Church governance. His rise in the Church culminated in his election as pope in **1265**, following the death of Pope Urban IV.

Papal Election: When Guido was elected as **Pope Clement IV**, it was a reflection of the Church's recognition of his strong leadership qualities and administrative capabilities. Despite his relatively short time as a cardinal, his reputation for wisdom, piety, and legal knowledge made him an ideal candidate during a time of political and ecclesiastical tension. His experience as a layman, lawyer, and father brought a unique perspective to his papacy, which emphasized the practical governance of the Church and the resolution of political conflicts.

Clement IV's unusual background as a family man and lawyer before his ordination gave him a distinct approach to the papacy, one that valued diplomacy, legal resolution, and governance. His papacy, though relatively short, was marked by his efforts to mediate political conflicts and strengthen the Church's position in Europe. His journey from a noble family life to the highest office in the Catholic Church remains a remarkable chapter in papal history.

In conclusion, Pope Clement IV's life before his ordination was defined by his marriage, his role as a father, and his successful career as a lawyer. His transition from a layman to a priest, bishop, and eventually pope after the death of his wife highlights a profound personal transformation and commitment to the Church. His unique background set him apart from other popes, bringing a wealth of life experience to his papacy that shaped his leadership and approach to governance.

Scandals and Exploits

POPE CLEMENT IV IS generally regarded as one of the more pious and morally upright pontiffs of the medieval era. Unlike many of his predecessors and successors, he avoided scandalous behavior and lived a life marked by personal integrity and devotion to the Church. However, despite his relatively clean record during his papacy, his **early family ties** and how they influenced his rise to power and leadership are still worth examining, as they provide insight into the political dynamics of the time and the delicate balancing act between secular and religious authority.

Family Ties and Influence: Before becoming pope, Clement IV (born **Guido le Gros**) was married and had children, a rare occurrence for a future pontiff. His early life as a husband and father, as well as his later entry into the priesthood, made him unique among the popes of the Middle Ages. Although he embraced a celibate and devout life following the death of his wife, the existence of his daughters raised questions about how he handled his personal relationships and whether these family connections influenced his papal decisions.

His daughters, after their mother's death, were sent to convents where they became nuns. While this decision reflected Clement's commitment to ensuring their spiritual well-being, it also had practical benefits for him as he moved into ecclesiastical roles. By placing his daughters in religious life, Clement ensured that they would not pose a threat to his position as a high-ranking Church leader, avoiding any potential accusations of nepotism or the kind of favoritism that had plagued the papacy in earlier periods.

Political and Secular Influence: Despite leading a pious life, Clement IV's papacy was not entirely free from political entanglements related to his family background. Clement was deeply involved in navigating the power struggles between the **French crown** and the **Holy Roman Empire**, two of the most dominant forces in Europe at the time. His close ties to **King Louis IX of France**, with whom he had developed a strong relationship during his earlier clerical career, were a crucial aspect of his papacy. While his relationship with the French crown provided him with political support, it also raised questions about whether his decisions were influenced by his loyalty to his homeland and its rulers.

Clement IV's French heritage and his connection to the French royal family played a role in several key political decisions during his papacy, most notably in his support for **Charles of Anjou**, the brother of King Louis IX, in his bid to become King of Sicily. Clement's backing of Charles was a highly significant and controversial move, as it shifted the balance of power in the region and led to the eventual defeat of the **Hohenstaufen dynasty**, which had long controlled the Kingdom of Sicily. This decision, while framed as a necessary political move to stabilize southern Italy and protect papal interests, was also seen by some as a reflection of Clement's personal ties to the French monarchy.

While Clement IV's support for Charles of Anjou was not scandalous in the same sense as the personal excesses of other popes, it did raise concerns about how much his early family connections influenced his actions as pope. By elevating Charles to power, Clement strengthened France's influence in European politics and further embedded the papacy in the secular affairs of kingdoms and dynasties. This move had long-lasting consequences, particularly in the context of the **Sicilian Vespers** rebellion that followed Charles' rule.

Handling Nepotism and Favoritism: One of the key areas where Clement IV avoided scandal was in his rejection of nepotism, a practice that had plagued many papacies. Despite his familial connections and the potential to favor his relatives, Clement made a conscious effort to avoid giving his daughters or other family members positions of power within the Church. This was a significant departure from the actions of many earlier popes, who often appointed nephews, brothers, and other relatives to influential positions, leading to widespread corruption.

Clement's decision to distance himself from his family, particularly after entering the priesthood, demonstrated his commitment to Church reform and the restoration of moral authority in the papal office. By ensuring that his daughters entered convents and lived quiet religious lives, Clement effectively removed them from the political equation and avoided any perception of favoritism. His rejection of nepotism set a positive example for future pontiffs and helped to strengthen the papacy's spiritual credibility at a time when the Church was often seen as corrupt and overly entangled in secular affairs.

Conflicts with the Holy Roman Empire: Clement IV's papacy was also marked by his ongoing struggle with the Holy Roman Empire, particularly regarding the imperial influence over Church affairs in Italy. His support for Charles of Anjou's bid for the Kingdom of Sicily was part of a broader strategy to limit the power of the **Hohenstaufen dynasty**, which had long dominated Italy and interfered in papal matters. This struggle, while political in nature, also reflected Clement's desire to assert papal independence and reduce secular interference in Church governance.

In this sense, Clement IV's early experiences in both the secular world and his family life may have influenced his approach to papal leadership. His background as a lawyer and nobleman gave him insight into the political dynamics of Europe, allowing him to navigate the complex relationships between the Church, monarchs, and noble families. His decision to support Charles of Anjou was driven by a desire to protect the papacy from imperial domination, but it also reflected the lasting influence of his ties to the French crown.

Conclusion: While Pope Clement IV's life after his ordination was relatively free of personal scandal, his early family ties and political connections continued to shape his papacy. His background as a husband and father, as well as his close relationship with the French monarchy, influenced key decisions during his tenure, particularly in his support for Charles of Anjou and his efforts to curb imperial influence over the Church. However, Clement's rejection of nepotism and his commitment to moral leadership helped distinguish him from more scandal-ridden pontiffs and contributed to his legacy as a pious and reform-minded pope. His ability to navigate the complex world of medieval politics while maintaining his personal integrity remains a notable aspect of his papacy.

Corruption

POPE CLEMENT IV'S PAPACY is generally remembered for its piety and integrity, especially in comparison to the more scandal-ridden papacies of the medieval period. However, his past as a **married man** before ordination, and his relatively late entry into the priesthood, created unique circumstances that could have impacted perceptions of his **papal authority**. While Clement IV was by no means corrupt, his personal background—particularly his marriage—may have influenced how he was viewed by contemporaries and contributed to subtle tensions in his role as pope.

Perceptions of His Past Marriage: Unlike most popes, who typically rose through the ranks of the Church as monks, clerics, or cardinals, **Guido le Gros** (Clement IV) had lived the life of a **nobleman, husband**, and **father** before his ordination. His wife's name remains largely unknown, but his daughters, whom he ensured were placed in convents, continued to live as nuns during his papacy. The fact that Clement had experienced secular family life, especially in an era when clerical celibacy was strictly enforced, undoubtedly shaped the way others perceived him, even if his past was not marked by any scandal or immoral behavior.

His past marriage might have been seen as a reminder of his former ties to the **lay world**, making him somewhat unconventional in the eyes of those who expected popes to have spent their entire lives within the Church. In a time when the Church emphasized clerical celibacy as a crucial marker of moral and spiritual authority, the fact that Clement had once been a married man could have raised questions about his eligibility to hold the highest ecclesiastical office, even though he fully embraced celibacy after his wife's death.

Clement IV's background might have also fostered some skepticism among more conservative factions within the Church, particularly those who believed that a pope's entire life should be devoted to religious service. While there was no outright challenge to his authority, there may have been a perception that his personal experience as a father and husband gave him a different, perhaps more worldly, perspective than other popes, many of whom had entered the Church at a young age.

Challenges to Celibacy: Clement IV's personal history as a married man brought into focus the Church's teachings on celibacy, which had been a topic of contention and reform for centuries. His experience raised delicate questions about how marriage and family life intersected with clerical responsibilities. While Clement never openly challenged the doctrine of celibacy, his past life as a husband may have made some critics uneasy about how his personal experiences aligned with the Church's strict stance on the matter.

At the same time, his successful transition from layman and father to priest and pope may have strengthened his reputation as a figure of moral integrity, someone who had lived both sides of life—secular and religious—and still chose to dedicate himself fully to the Church after his wife's death. Nevertheless, the contrast between his earlier life and the rigid expectations of celibacy for priests and popes could have left some questioning his past, even if there were no direct accusations of impropriety.

French Royal Connections and Allegiances: In addition to his marriage and family life, Clement IV's close ties to **France**, particularly to **King Louis IX** and the **Capetian dynasty**, may have complicated his papal authority. His rise to power was supported by his strong connection to the French crown, which gave him influence but also exposed him to concerns that his loyalty might be divided. His support for **Charles of Anjou**, Louis IX's brother, in claiming the **Kingdom of Sicily**, was seen as politically motivated and raised concerns that Clement was more beholden to French interests than to the broader mission of the Church.

While Clement's intentions in backing Charles of Anjou were largely driven by political necessity—namely to counter the power of the **Hohenstaufen dynasty** and secure the papal states—this decision also invited accusations that his past alliances and family ties to the French monarchy influenced his governance. The fact that Clement IV had come from a noble family and lived as a layman before becoming pope may have heightened suspicions that he was too closely tied to secular powers.

Corruption-Free Legacy Amid Political Compromises: Compared to other medieval popes, Clement IV was largely free of personal corruption. He was known for his piety, dedication to reform, and commitment to the Church's moral authority. However, the very fact that he had once been married and had children set him apart from other popes and may have led to a perception that he was somewhat compromised by his past.

His decision to place his daughters in convents ensured that they would not become pawns in the political or ecclesiastical games of the time, but the existence of his family, however well-managed, could have been seen as a subtle challenge to the idea of papal celibacy and purity. His refusal to engage in nepotism—especially notable given the widespread practice of appointing family members to powerful Church positions—was a testament to his integrity, but his past family life still colored perceptions of his papacy.

In conclusion, while Pope Clement IV's papacy was marked by personal piety and a lack of corruption, his past as a married man and father likely influenced how some viewed his authority. Though he successfully navigated the challenges of leading the Church without succumbing to nepotism or scandal, his background raised subtle questions about the intersection of his secular past and the strict expectations of papal leadership. His life before ordination, though not scandalous in itself, may have shaped the political and spiritual dynamics of his papacy in ways that are important to consider, especially in the context of medieval views on clerical celibacy and the Church's relationship with secular powers.

Handling His Family

POPE CLEMENT IV, BORN **Guido le Gros**, faced a unique challenge in managing his family ties during his papacy, particularly given his past as a **husband** and **father** before entering the Church. Unlike most popes, who had spent their entire lives within the clerical sphere, Clement had two daughters from his marriage. To ensure that his papacy remained free from any accusations of nepotism or scandal, Clement IV took careful steps to manage his family, particularly by ensuring that his daughters became **nuns**, effectively removing them from the political and ecclesiastical landscape. This decision allowed him to maintain the integrity of his papal office while adhering to the Church's moral and ethical expectations.

The Decision to Send His Daughters to Convents: After the death of his wife, Guido le Gros chose to enter the priesthood, making a dramatic shift from his previous life as a layman, husband, and father. His daughters, who were left without their mother, became his responsibility to manage within the context of his new spiritual path. By ensuring that his daughters entered convents and embraced a religious life as nuns, Clement IV effectively shielded them—and himself—from any potential controversy that might have arisen due to their familial connections to the pope.

The placement of his daughters in convents was a strategic move that allowed Clement to fully commit to his spiritual and clerical duties without being distracted by familial obligations. It also preemptively addressed any concerns about **nepotism** or favoritism, which had been major issues for other popes. In a time when many popes were criticized for appointing family members to influential Church positions or allowing them to meddle in papal affairs, Clement's decision to remove his daughters from the political and social spheres was seen as a clear indication of his integrity and dedication to reform.

Avoiding Scandal and Nepotism: The issue of nepotism had plagued the papacy for centuries, with many popes appointing their sons, nephews, or other relatives to positions of power within the Church. This often led to corruption, favoritism, and a weakening of the Church's moral authority. By ensuring that his daughters became nuns, Clement IV avoided any possibility of being accused of using his papal office to advance his family's interests. This was a sharp departure from the practices of previous popes, many of whom had been heavily criticized for allowing their family members to wield undue influence.

Clement IV's approach also helped him maintain his reputation as a reform-minded pope, particularly at a time when the Church was in need of moral and administrative reform. By keeping his daughters in religious life, Clement sent a strong message that he was not willing to compromise the spiritual purity of his office for personal gain. This move further distanced him from the secular ambitions that often accompanied papal appointments, reinforcing his commitment to the Church's mission.

Securing His Daughters' Spiritual Lives: Beyond the political and practical considerations, Clement IV's decision to send his daughters to convents may also have been motivated by genuine concern for their spiritual well-being. As a man who had experienced both secular and religious life, Clement likely saw the convent as a place where his daughters could live out their faith in a protected, stable environment. Their decision to become nuns not only helped Clement manage his papal responsibilities without distraction but also ensured that his daughters would be cared for within the Church's structure.

Clement IV's background as a married man could have posed complications during his papacy, but his careful handling of his family ensured that no such controversies arose. By committing his daughters to religious life, he demonstrated both his personal piety and his understanding of the need for discretion in managing familial connections to the papacy. His daughters' positions as nuns effectively removed them from public view and any potential political entanglements that could have undermined his papal authority.

Long-Term Impact on the Papacy: Clement IV's decision to distance his family from his papal duties by placing his daughters in convents set an important precedent for future popes. His handling of his family was a significant departure from the nepotism and favoritism that had characterized many previous papacies. By choosing not to involve his family in Church matters, Clement helped reinforce the idea that the papacy should be free from secular interference and personal ambition, contributing to the broader movement for Church reform.

In conclusion, Pope Clement IV managed his family with great care, ensuring that his daughters entered convents and became nuns, which effectively removed any potential controversy or scandal surrounding their relationship to the pope. By doing so, Clement avoided the pitfalls of nepotism that had plagued many of his predecessors, maintaining the integrity of his papal office. His decision to distance his family from Church politics allowed him to focus on his duties as pope while reinforcing his commitment to the moral and spiritual authority of the Church.

7. Pope Pius II (1458–1464)

Life and Background

Pope Pius II, born **Enea Silvio Piccolomini** on **October 18, 1405,** in Corsignano, Italy (later renamed **Pienza** in his honor), led an extraordinary and multifaceted life before becoming pope. His early years were marked by his career as a **humanist scholar**, diplomat, and writer, during a time when Renaissance humanism was flourishing across Europe. Before entering the priesthood, Pius II lived a life that was more typical of a Renaissance courtier than a future pope, even fathering **children** during his youth. His background as a humanist and his secular experiences shaped much of his intellectual approach and leadership as pope.

Early Life and Education: Enea Silvio Piccolomini was born into a noble but impoverished family, one of 18 children. Despite the family's lack of wealth, the Piccolominis were well connected within the Sienese nobility, which allowed young Enea Silvio to pursue an education. He studied at the **University of Siena** and later at the **University of Florence**, where he was exposed to the blossoming intellectual movement of **Renaissance humanism**. During this period, humanist scholars emphasized the study of classical antiquity, literature, and the exploration of human potential, all of which left a lasting mark on Piccolomini's thinking.

His education in classical languages and literature, philosophy, and rhetoric enabled him to become a prominent figure in the humanist circles of Italy. He was well-versed in Latin and Greek and developed a reputation as a skilled writer and orator. This intellectual foundation would later serve him well in both his diplomatic and ecclesiastical careers.

Diplomatic and Secular Career: Before entering the priesthood, Enea Silvio Piccolomini embarked on a career as a **diplomat** and **secretary** for various prominent figures, including the **Cardinal of Siena** and the **Holy Roman Emperor Frederick III**. His secular career took him across Europe, where he was involved in a variety of political and diplomatic missions. During his time as a diplomat, he traveled extensively to countries such as Scotland, England, Germany, and the court of the Pope in Rome, gaining firsthand experience in the complex political and ecclesiastical power dynamics of the 15th century.

Throughout this period, Piccolomini's personal life was far from the piety expected of a future pope. Like many Renaissance humanists, he embraced the courtly lifestyle and had several romantic entanglements, fathering at least **two illegitimate children**—a son, **Giovanni**, and a daughter, **Maria**—by different women. This aspect of his early life was not uncommon among Renaissance scholars and courtiers, but it stood in stark contrast to the expectations of celibacy and moral restraint that came with his later role as pope.

Humanist Scholar and Writer: In addition to his diplomatic work, Piccolomini became a renowned **humanist writer**. He authored a wide range of works, including poetry, letters, historical writings, and plays. His most famous literary work was his **autobiography**, written while he was pope, titled *Commentaries*, which is notable for being one of the first autobiographies ever written by a pope. In it, he candidly described his early life, including his romantic affairs and his secular ambitions, providing a rare glimpse into the personal thoughts of a Renaissance pope.

His humanist writings, especially his passion for classical literature, brought him into contact with some of the leading intellectual figures of his time. Piccolomini became an advocate of humanist ideals, blending classical knowledge with Christian values, and these intellectual pursuits influenced his views on education, governance, and diplomacy during his papacy.

Entry into the Church and Rise to the Papacy: Enea Silvio Piccolomini's turn toward the Church came later in life, after years of diplomatic service. In **1445**, at the age of 40, he was ordained as a priest. His transition into the Church was not solely motivated by spiritual conviction but also by his realization of the political power and influence the Church wielded in European affairs. Piccolomini quickly rose through the ecclesiastical ranks, becoming **Bishop of Trieste** in 1447 and **Bishop of Siena** in 1449. His talents as a diplomat and writer continued to serve him well, and in **1456**, he was appointed **Cardinal** by **Pope Calixtus III**.

In **1458**, following the death of Pope Calixtus III, Piccolomini was elected pope, taking the name **Pius II**. His election was largely due to his reputation as a skilled diplomat and his extensive knowledge of European politics. As pope, Pius II sought to balance the spiritual responsibilities of his office with his humanist ideals, which emphasized the importance of education, classical knowledge, and diplomacy.

Legacy of His Early Life: Pope Pius II's early life as a humanist scholar and diplomat, as well as his experience as a father, gave him a unique perspective that set him apart from other popes. His secular past, including his romantic relationships and the children he fathered, was well known and somewhat controversial. However, his candid admission of his past, especially in his autobiography, allowed him to own his earlier life and focus on his papal duties with a sense of pragmatism.

While his earlier life could have been seen as a liability, Pius II's experiences in the secular world contributed to his success as a pope. His deep understanding of diplomacy, politics, and the intellectual currents of the Renaissance allowed him to navigate the complexities of the Church's role in Europe during a time of great change. His reign was marked by efforts to unite Christian Europe against the advancing Ottoman Empire and to reform the Church, though his plans for a crusade ultimately fell short.

In conclusion, Pope Pius II's early life as Enea Silvio Piccolomini was filled with intellectual pursuits, diplomatic service, and personal experiences that were unconventional for a future pope. His humanist scholarship and experience as a father shaped his papacy in ways that reflected the Renaissance values of learning, diplomacy, and a nuanced understanding of human nature. Though his early life included romantic entanglements and secular ambitions, his papacy was marked by a genuine commitment to the Church's mission and a recognition of the changing world in which it operated.

Scandals and Exploits

POPE PIUS II, BORN **Enea Silvio Piccolomini**, was a Renaissance figure who embodied the complexity of the time, including its humanistic embrace of personal experience and classical ideals. One of the most striking and unusual aspects of his papacy was his **frankness** about his past, particularly his **sexual exploits**, which he detailed in his **autobiography**, *Commentaries*. This openness about his early life, including his romantic entanglements and fathering illegitimate children, was a rarity for a pope and marked a sharp contrast with the more traditional expectations of papal decorum. His candid admission of his past both shocked and intrigued contemporaries and has contributed to the lasting complexity of his reputation.

Frank Admissions in His Autobiography: Pius II was unique among popes in writing an **autobiography**, *Commentaries*, in which he provided a detailed account of his life, including his secular experiences before his ordination. In these writings, he openly discussed his youthful indiscretions, including **romantic affairs** and his fathering of at least **two illegitimate children**—a son named Giovanni and a daughter named Maria. These relationships occurred during his time as a **humanist scholar**, diplomat, and secretary to powerful figures across Europe, well before his entry into the Church. His experiences, recounted with surprising honesty, reveal the personal struggles of a man who lived as a courtier and humanist before embracing the priesthood.

This candor was highly unusual for a pope, as the papal office traditionally emphasized moral authority, purity, and spiritual leadership. Yet Pius II did not shy away from discussing his past failings. In one of the more famous passages of his *Commentaries*, he described himself as a young man who "sought pleasure" and indulged in the worldly temptations of court life. This openness was reflective of the

Renaissance humanist ethos, which encouraged individuals to explore the fullness of human experience, including both virtues and vices.

Impact on His Reputation: The admission of his youthful exploits had a mixed effect on Pius II's reputation. For some contemporaries, particularly within the Church, his openness about his sexual past was troubling, as it seemed at odds with the moral authority expected of a pope. His frank acknowledgment of fathering children outside of marriage, as well as his many affairs, could have been seen as undermining his credibility as a spiritual leader.

However, Pius II's candidness also had a certain appeal, especially among the more **humanist-minded intellectuals** of his time. His willingness to admit his flaws and acknowledge his secular past made him a relatable figure, embodying the Renaissance idea that individuals could grow, learn, and transform through their life experiences. By laying bare his past, Pius II portrayed himself as a man who had overcome personal failings to become a leader of the Church. In this way, his personal story became one of redemption and renewal, themes that resonated with many Renaissance thinkers who valued human growth and self-realization.

Moreover, Pius II's candid admissions allowed him to frame his papacy as a period of reform and dedication to spiritual duties, following a period of personal missteps. His past did not seem to hinder his ability to function as an effective pope; if anything, it added a level of **pragmatism** to his leadership. He was, after all, a man who understood both the secular world and the spiritual calling of the Church, a combination that allowed him to navigate the political complexities of the time.

Challenges and Criticism: Despite his humanist credentials and his ability to leverage his past into a narrative of personal growth, there were certainly those within the Church who saw his admissions as problematic. Conservative factions within the papal court and other more devout members of the clergy were uncomfortable with the idea of a pope openly discussing his past sexual exploits. The image of the pope as the supreme moral leader of the Christian world was central to the Church's authority, and any deviation from this ideal was viewed with suspicion.

Additionally, there was a broader concern about the moral authority of the papacy during this period. The Renaissance popes were often criticized for their secular indulgences and political entanglements, and Pius II's past could have been used by his critics as further evidence that the Church had lost its way. While Pius II's reforms and diplomatic efforts were largely respected, his past indiscretions served as fodder for those who sought to highlight the moral laxity of the papacy during the Renaissance.

Legacy of Honesty and Humanism: In the long run, Pius II's willingness to openly discuss his sexual past in his autobiography became part of his larger legacy as a **Renaissance pope**. His admissions did not overshadow his accomplishments as pope, which included efforts to organize a crusade against the **Ottoman Empire**, his diplomatic missions, and his literary contributions. His intellectual curiosity, his literary talent, and his deep understanding of European politics made him one of the most well-rounded and culturally significant popes of his time.

Pius II's autobiography, with its frank reflections on his past, has become a valuable historical document that provides insight into the mind of a Renaissance humanist who ascended to the highest office of the Church. His honesty, while unconventional, speaks to a broader cultural shift in which human experience, in all its complexity, was acknowledged and even celebrated.

In conclusion, Pope Pius II's admission of his past sexual exploits, including fathering children, was a rare and surprising move for a pope. His candidness in his *Commentaries* affected his reputation in both positive and negative ways, with some viewing his openness as a mark of humanist self-awareness and others seeing it as a challenge to the moral authority of the papacy. Ultimately, Pius II's ability to frame his early life as a journey of growth and redemption allowed him to reconcile his secular past with his papal duties, making him a unique figure in the history of the papacy.

Corruption

ALTHOUGH **Pope Pius II** is generally remembered as a capable leader and a figure of Renaissance humanism, his earlier life stands in stark contrast to the **celibate expectations** of the papacy. Before his ordination, Pius II (born **Enea Silvio Piccolomini**) led a very different life, embracing the worldly pleasures of a **courtier, diplomat**, and **humanist scholar**. He fathered **illegitimate children**, engaged in romantic affairs, and lived a lifestyle that, while not uncommon for Renaissance intellectuals, clashed with the ideals of priestly celibacy and moral purity that the Church demanded of its leaders. This contrast between his early life and the celibate expectations of the papal office offers a fascinating window into the complexities of Pius II's character and leadership.

Early Life and Secular Indulgences: Pius II's pre-papal life was filled with activities that were directly at odds with the celibate and morally restrained image expected of a pope. As a young man, he pursued **romantic relationships** and fathered at least two illegitimate children—one by a woman in Strasbourg and another by a Scottish woman while he was on a diplomatic mission to Scotland. These affairs were not hidden or secretive; in fact, Pius II openly admitted to them later in his life, even acknowledging his children and his youthful indiscretions in his famous autobiography, *Commentaries*.

This lifestyle reflected the broader cultural environment of the **Renaissance**, where humanist scholars, writers, and courtiers often embraced a more worldly and secular approach to life. Piccolomini was part of this movement, living as a diplomat, poet, and humanist before he entered the Church. His interactions with the courts of Europe, where indulgence in sensual pleasures and romantic exploits were common, shaped his early experiences. However, this was a direct contrast to the strict celibacy required of clerics, particularly the pope.

Contrast with Papal Expectations: The **papacy** during the 15th century, although at times marked by political maneuvering and personal ambition, was still supposed to be a position of **moral and spiritual authority**. Popes were expected to embody the virtues of humility, celibacy, and moral purity. When Enea Silvio Piccolomini was elected **Pope Pius II** in **1458**, his past did not disqualify him, but it certainly created an unusual dynamic between the man he had been and the role he now assumed.

As pope, Pius II upheld the Church's expectations of celibacy and moral conduct, but his earlier life was a reminder of the human complexities behind the papal office. In particular, his candid admission of his youthful behavior was striking. While he did not try to conceal his past, his decision to publicly acknowledge it—most notably in his autobiography—stood in stark contrast to the more conservative attitudes that traditionally surrounded the papacy.

His admission, while refreshing in its honesty, raised questions about how seriously the celibacy requirement could be taken for a pope who had not always adhered to it. By the time he became pope, Pius II had long since abandoned his youthful indiscretions, but the fact that he had fathered children and led a courtly lifestyle remained an indelible part of his public image.

Impact on Perception of the Papacy: Although Pius II was considered less corrupt than some of his predecessors and contemporaries, particularly the notorious Renaissance popes like **Alexander VI**, his earlier life presented a challenge to the **celibate ideal** of the papal office. His transparency about his youthful exploits was in some ways admirable, but it also added to the sense that the papacy was increasingly intertwined with worldly concerns, rather than being purely a spiritual institution.

For more conservative factions within the Church, Pius II's background may have been a source of discomfort. After all, his rise to the papal throne was emblematic of a broader trend during the

Renaissance, where **humanist ideals** and secular experiences began to blend with religious leadership. While Pius II reformed his behavior as he moved deeper into the Church, his past could still be seen as a lingering contradiction to the moral standards expected of the pope.

Nevertheless, Pius II's earlier life did not result in a reputation for personal corruption during his papacy. Unlike popes who openly engaged in corrupt practices such as simony (the selling of Church offices) or moral excesses while in office, Pius II's time as pope was marked by **diplomatic efforts**, a focus on **reforming the Church**, and attempts to organize a **crusade** against the Ottoman Turks. His earlier life, however, remained a contrast to the celibate and morally upright figure he became as the head of the Church.

Legacy and Interpretation: Pius II's legacy is defined by the tension between his **secular past** and his role as a religious leader. On one hand, his experience as a diplomat and humanist scholar made him a highly effective leader, deeply knowledgeable about European politics and capable of navigating complex diplomatic relationships. On the other hand, his early romantic relationships and fathering of children clashed with the image of celibacy and moral purity that was central to the papacy.

Ultimately, Pius II managed to maintain his reputation as a capable and reform-minded pope, but his earlier life serves as a reminder of the **human complexity** behind the papal office. His candidness about his past, while refreshing in its honesty, revealed the struggles that could exist between the **secular and spiritual worlds**. While his early life was a far cry from the celibate expectations of the papacy, his ability to navigate both worlds and transform himself into a religious leader is part of what makes him one of the more interesting figures in papal history.

In conclusion, while Pius II was less corrupt than some of his papal contemporaries, his early life presented a notable contrast to the celibate and morally pure expectations of the papacy. His frankness about his youthful indiscretions, including fathering children, added complexity to his legacy, but did not overshadow his accomplishments as pope. His ability to reconcile his past with his papal responsibilities highlights the unique challenges he faced as both a Renaissance humanist and a spiritual leader of the Catholic Church.

Handling His Family

POPE PIUS II, BORN **Enea Silvio Piccolomini**, had a complex personal history that included romantic relationships and fathering **illegitimate children** before his entry into the Church. As he transitioned from a secular life into the priesthood and eventually the papacy, Pius II took deliberate steps to distance himself from his past relationships and manage the potential complications posed by his children. His handling of these personal matters was crucial in maintaining his papal authority and credibility while navigating the expectations of celibacy and moral purity that came with the papal office.

Distancing from Past Relationships: Before his ordination, Enea Silvio Piccolomini had lived as a **humanist scholar** and diplomat, indulging in the romantic freedoms often associated with Renaissance courtiers. He had relationships with multiple women, including a long-term affair with a woman in Strasbourg and another romantic involvement in Scotland, both of which resulted in the birth of illegitimate children. While such behavior was not uncommon for secular intellectuals of the time, it posed a potential problem when Piccolomini transitioned into the Church.

Upon deciding to pursue the priesthood, Pius II began to distance himself from these relationships. His journey into the Church marked a clear break with his earlier life, and he publicly acknowledged his youthful indiscretions, which was a rare display of **candor** for someone in his position. Rather than attempting to conceal his past, Pius II addressed it openly in his writings, particularly in his autobiography, *Commentaries*, where he reflected on his personal failings. This honesty, while unusual, helped him confront his past head-on and demonstrate that he had moved beyond his former lifestyle.

By acknowledging his past openly, Pius II effectively neutralized potential scandals. His forthrightness allowed him to own his past rather than be subjected to rumors or speculation. It also helped to frame his life as one of **redemption**—a narrative of a man who had embraced a new calling and left behind the indulgences of his younger years.

Managing His Children: The most significant challenge Pius II faced in terms of his family was how to manage the existence of his two **illegitimate children**—a son, **Giovanni**, and a daughter, **Maria**. While having children was not inherently scandalous for a secular courtier, it presented a complication for a man ascending to the papacy, where celibacy and the absence of personal familial ties were central expectations.

Pius II's handling of his children was pragmatic. He did not publicly deny their existence but instead ensured that they were cared for outside of the public eye, minimizing their influence on his clerical career. His son Giovanni was placed into the care of trusted guardians, and his daughter Maria entered a convent. By having Maria become a nun, Pius II followed a common practice of the time, where illegitimate daughters were often sent to religious institutions to live a quiet and respectable life, thus removing them from political or social entanglements.

The decision to send Maria to a convent not only ensured her welfare but also distanced her from her father's rising position in the Church. This move likely helped to prevent any accusations of **nepotism** or favoritism that might have emerged had she remained more closely tied to his clerical duties. By keeping his children at a distance, Pius II maintained the separation between his papal responsibilities and his personal life, allowing him to focus on the spiritual leadership required of his office.

Balancing Personal Honesty and Papal Expectations: Pius II's transition from a father and humanist scholar to the leader of the Catholic Church required careful management of both his past and his family. While his candidness about his former relationships and children was unusual for a pope, it helped establish a clear distinction between his earlier life and his papal role. He did not try to erase his past but instead framed it as a youthful phase that he had outgrown, underscoring the transformative power of his commitment to the Church.

This approach allowed Pius II to handle his family without compromising his authority as pope. By acknowledging his children but ensuring they did not interfere with his clerical duties, he effectively managed the delicate balance between his personal history and the expectations of celibacy and moral leadership. His pragmatic decisions regarding his children, especially his daughter's placement in a convent, helped minimize any potential scandals and avoided the perception that he was using his papal position to benefit his family.

Conclusion: Pope Pius II's handling of his family, particularly his children from past relationships, was marked by careful distance and pragmatic decisions. His openness about his youthful indiscretions, combined with his efforts to separate his personal life from his role as pope, allowed him to navigate the expectations of celibacy and moral purity while avoiding scandal. By sending his daughter to a convent and keeping his son away from papal affairs, Pius II ensured that his family did not interfere with his papacy, maintaining his reputation as a capable and reform-minded leader of the Church. His ability to balance these personal and public responsibilities is a testament to his skill in managing the complexities of both his past and his role as pope.

8. Pope Innocent VIII (1484–1492)

Life and Background

Pope Innocent VIII, born **Giovanni Battista Cybo** on **February 24, 1432**, in Genoa, Italy, rose to the papacy during one of the most politically charged and morally controversial periods in the history of the Catholic Church. His papacy is often associated with **nepotism** and the use of papal power to advance his family's interests, particularly through his children, **Franceschetto Cybo** and **Teodorina Cybo**, who played significant roles during his tenure as pope. Innocent VIII's rise to power and his subsequent actions highlight the challenges of navigating familial loyalty while managing the responsibilities of the papal office.

Early Life and Career: Giovanni Battista Cybo came from a prominent Genoese family with ties to both the nobility and the clergy. His father, **Arano Cybo**, served as viceroy of Naples, and his mother was of Greek descent, a connection that provided the young Giovanni with valuable social and political contacts. After studying in **Padua** and **Rome**, Cybo entered the Church, where his family's influence helped him secure various clerical positions.

Cybo's ecclesiastical career advanced steadily, and in **1467**, he was appointed **bishop of Savona** by **Pope Paul II**. His rise continued under **Pope Sixtus IV**, who elevated him to the rank of **cardinal** in **1473**, a move that brought him closer to the inner workings of the Vatican. Cybo's charm, diplomacy, and powerful family connections helped him navigate the complex politics of the Roman Curia, and when Pope Sixtus IV died in 1484, Cybo emerged as a strong contender for the papal throne.

Election as Pope: Cybo's election as **Pope Innocent VIII** on **August 29, 1484**, was largely a result of political maneuvering and compromise among the College of Cardinals. Innocent VIII was seen as a conciliatory figure who could bridge the divisions within the Curia and maintain stability in the increasingly turbulent Italian political landscape. However, his papacy was immediately marked by his efforts to consolidate power and secure advantages for his family, particularly through the actions of his illegitimate children.

Franceschetto Cybo: One of the most significant figures during Innocent VIII's papacy was his son, **Franceschetto Cybo**, who benefited immensely from his father's influence. Franceschetto was born out of wedlock before Giovanni Battista Cybo entered the Church, but Innocent VIII made no efforts to distance himself from his son upon becoming pope. Instead, he openly acknowledged Franceschetto and used his papal power to enrich and elevate him within Italian society.

Franceschetto's presence at the Vatican was a major source of controversy, as Innocent VIII showered him with wealth and titles, engaging in **nepotism** on an unprecedented scale. Franceschetto was known for his gambling and lavish lifestyle, which earned him a reputation for wastefulness and greed. To secure his son's position, Innocent VIII arranged a politically advantageous marriage between Franceschetto and **Maddalena de' Medici**, the daughter of **Lorenzo de' Medici**, the powerful ruler of Florence. This alliance between the Cybo and Medici families solidified Franceschetto's standing and strengthened Innocent VIII's ties to Florence.

Franceschetto's marriage to Maddalena de' Medici was a critical step in securing the family's political future. The Cybo-Medici alliance gave Innocent VIII significant influence in Florence and bolstered his position within the Italian political landscape. However,

Franceschetto's continued indulgence in gambling and reckless spending remained a point of concern, as it contrasted with the spiritual and moral leadership expected of the papacy.

Teodorina Cybo: In addition to Franceschetto, Innocent VIII had a daughter, **Teodorina Cybo**, whose role during his papacy also underscored the use of family ties to consolidate power. Although Teodorina played a more private role compared to her brother, her marriage into a prominent noble family helped strengthen the Cybo family's connections. She married **Gerardo Usodimare**, a Genoese nobleman, further cementing the Cybo family's influence in northern Italy.

While Teodorina's public presence was less controversial than Franceschetto's, her marriage was part of Innocent VIII's broader strategy of using family alliances to secure the Cybo dynasty's position in Italian politics. Innocent VIII's willingness to promote his children's interests—despite the Church's official stance on celibacy—was indicative of the broader trends of nepotism that had come to characterize the papacy during this period.

Challenges and Criticism: Innocent VIII's overt nepotism and his efforts to elevate his children were not without their critics. Many within the Church saw his actions as a corruption of the papal office, which was supposed to be dedicated to spiritual leadership rather than familial gain. The fact that Innocent VIII openly supported his illegitimate children while ignoring the celibacy requirement of the priesthood was a clear violation of Church doctrine, leading to accusations of hypocrisy and moral compromise.

In addition to nepotism, Innocent VIII's papacy was marked by other controversial actions, including his issuing of the papal bull **Summis desiderantes affectibus** in 1484, which authorized the persecution of witches in Germany. This decree contributed to the rise of witch hunts in Europe, further tarnishing Innocent VIII's legacy as a pope more focused on political and personal gain than on spiritual matters.

Legacy: Despite the criticisms surrounding his papacy, Innocent VIII's influence on Italian politics and his strengthening of the Cybo family's position were significant. His son Franceschetto, through his marriage to Maddalena de' Medici, became linked to one of the most powerful families in Renaissance Italy, ensuring that the Cybo name would remain prominent in the region's political affairs for years to come. His daughter Teodorina's marriage similarly contributed to the family's political connections.

Innocent VIII's legacy, however, is largely defined by his nepotism and his use of papal power to benefit his children. While he was less notorious than some of his more corrupt successors, such as **Pope Alexander VI**, his actions set a precedent for the use of the papal office as a tool for personal and familial advancement.

In conclusion, Pope Innocent VIII's rise to power and his papacy were deeply intertwined with his efforts to elevate his children, Franceschetto and Teodorina Cybo. By leveraging his papal authority to secure advantageous marriages and political alliances, Innocent VIII exemplified the trend of nepotism that characterized the Renaissance papacy. While his children's roles helped to solidify the Cybo family's power, they also contributed to the perception of Innocent VIII as a pope more concerned with personal gain than with the spiritual leadership of the Church.

Scandals and Exploits

POPE INNOCENT VIII'S papacy was notorious for its rampant **nepotism** and the blatant use of papal power to enrich his family, particularly his son, **Franceschetto Cybo**. Franceschetto became a central figure in the scandals that plagued Innocent's reign, as his extravagant lifestyle, penchant for gambling, and accumulation of wealth through papal favor drew widespread criticism. His actions, along with Innocent VIII's willingness to overlook them, tarnished the moral standing of the papacy and highlighted the corrupt practices that had taken hold of the Church during this period.

Nepotism and Favoritism: One of the major scandals involving Franceschetto Cybo was the **open nepotism** practiced by his father. Unlike many previous popes who fathered illegitimate children but kept their existence discreet, Innocent VIII openly acknowledged Franceschetto and placed him at the heart of his political strategy. Franceschetto, who had no significant talents or political acumen, was elevated to a position of immense power and wealth solely because of his father's influence. Innocent VIII bestowed upon him vast amounts of wealth and land, using Church resources to secure his son's financial future and social standing.

Franceschetto's marriage to **Maddalena de' Medici**, the daughter of **Lorenzo de' Medici**, was one of the clearest examples of this nepotism. The marriage, arranged by Innocent VIII, solidified an alliance between the Cybo and Medici families, giving Franceschetto a powerful political connection to one of the most influential families in Italy. This marriage, while politically advantageous, further entrenched the notion that Franceschetto was benefiting solely from his father's papal power, without any merit of his own.

Bribery and Wealth Accumulation: Another major scandal involving Franceschetto was his accumulation of vast wealth through **bribery** and the exploitation of Church offices. As the pope's son,

Franceschetto had access to the immense financial resources of the Church, and he did not hesitate to use this access for personal gain. He was notorious for accepting bribes in exchange for favors, including the selling of Church offices and appointments—an egregious form of **simony** that was rampant during his father's papacy.

Franceschetto's reputation for corruption became a source of public outrage, as he was seen as one of the most blatant examples of the papacy's moral decay. His **gambling habits** were well known, and much of the wealth he accumulated through bribes and Church resources was squandered on gambling debts. His reckless spending and financial mismanagement only further alienated the public and clergy, who saw him as a symbol of the papal office's corruption.

The accumulation of wealth through Church offices and bribes was not just a personal indulgence for Franceschetto but also a reflection of the broader corruption within Innocent VIII's papal administration. Innocent VIII's willingness to grant Franceschetto control over Church finances and offices, despite his son's lack of qualifications, contributed to the perception that the papacy was more concerned with personal and familial enrichment than with spiritual leadership.

Franceschetto's Extravagance: Franceschetto's extravagant lifestyle was another major source of scandal during Innocent VIII's papacy. He lived in luxury, thanks to the wealth and privileges bestowed upon him by his father. His gambling habits were notorious, and he was known to have amassed large debts that had to be covered by the Vatican's coffers. This extravagance, combined with his lack of any meaningful contributions to the Church or the political landscape, made him an object of derision and contempt.

Despite his father's best efforts to secure Franceschetto's future through wealth and political alliances, Franceschetto's profligate lifestyle continually undermined his status. He was seen as a liability to the papacy, draining its resources for personal gain while contributing nothing of value. His constant need for money to cover his gambling debts led him to engage in further corrupt practices, including the selling of Church offices and positions.

Political Exploits and Involvement in Intrigue: Franceschetto's involvement in political intrigue further complicated his relationship with the papacy. His marriage to Maddalena de' Medici gave him a connection to Florence's ruling family, which helped solidify Innocent VIII's political influence in the region. However, Franceschetto's lack of political savvy and his reputation as a gambler and spendthrift undermined his ability to take full advantage of this alliance. His political exploits were more the result of his father's influence than his own abilities, and he became entangled in various schemes that often ended in failure.

One of the most notable political moves involving Franceschetto was his involvement in the **arranged marriages** of his relatives to other prominent families. Innocent VIII sought to strengthen the Cybo family's power by arranging marriages between Franceschetto's relatives and influential noble families throughout Italy. While these marriages were intended to secure the family's influence, they were often overshadowed by Franceschetto's mismanagement and lack of leadership.

Public Backlash and Impact on Innocent VIII's Papacy: Franceschetto's scandals and exploits had a significant impact on Innocent VIII's papacy, damaging the reputation of the pope and the Church as a whole. The blatant nepotism, bribery, and wealth accumulation associated with Franceschetto made Innocent VIII's papacy a symbol of corruption, contributing to the growing calls for reform within the Church.

Innocent VIII's failure to rein in his son's behavior was seen as a major flaw in his leadership. The public perception of the papacy during this time was that it had become little more than a tool for personal enrichment, with Church offices and resources being exploited for the benefit of the pope's family. Franceschetto's scandals fueled the perception that the Church was in moral decline, and this perception would later play a role in the growing discontent that led to the **Protestant Reformation**.

In conclusion, Franceschetto Cybo's involvement in the scandals surrounding **nepotism**, **bribery**, and the accumulation of wealth severely damaged the moral standing of Pope Innocent VIII's papacy. Franceschetto's reckless spending, gambling habits, and corruption made him a symbol of the broader corruption that had taken hold of the Renaissance papacy. His actions, combined with Innocent VIII's willingness to indulge his son's ambitions, contributed to the public's growing disillusionment with the Church, leaving a legacy of scandal that overshadowed much of Innocent VIII's papacy.

Corruption

POPE INNOCENT VIII'S papacy was marked by rampant corruption, with his tenure often characterized by the widespread selling of **church offices**, indulgences, and the blatant use of papal power to **enrich his family**. Innocent VIII's reliance on nepotism and financial exploitation to secure the fortunes of his illegitimate children and close relatives contributed significantly to the moral decline of the Church during this period. His actions laid the groundwork for public disillusionment with the papacy, setting the stage for growing calls for reform that would culminate in the Protestant Reformation.

Selling of Church Offices (Simony): One of the most notorious forms of corruption during Innocent VIII's papacy was **simony**, the selling of church offices for money. Innocent VIII, like many Renaissance popes, used the immense power of the papal office to grant high-ranking positions within the Church to those who could afford them, often at the expense of qualified and devout candidates. This practice was seen as one of the greatest corruptions of the time, as it allowed wealthy individuals to purchase spiritual authority rather than earning it through merit or religious devotion.

The revenues from the sale of church offices were used to enrich Innocent VIII's family, particularly his son, **Franceschetto Cybo**, who became notorious for his extravagant lifestyle, gambling habits, and insatiable need for money. Franceschetto benefited directly from his father's corrupt practices, as the funds generated through simony were often funneled into his personal accounts to cover his mounting debts. Innocent VIII's decision to sell church offices for financial gain undermined the spiritual integrity of the Church, creating resentment among the clergy and laity alike.

Simony during Innocent VIII's reign was not limited to lower church positions but extended to influential and powerful offices such as bishoprics and cardinalships. Wealthy families across Europe saw church offices as valuable political tools, and Innocent VIII was more than willing to sell these positions to the highest bidders, regardless of the candidate's qualifications. This practice further eroded the moral authority of the Church, as positions that should have been reserved for devout and learned individuals were instead occupied by those motivated by wealth and status.

Indulgences and Financial Exploitation: Another key source of corruption during Innocent VIII's papacy was the sale of **indulgences**, a practice that allowed the Church to grant remission of sins in exchange for financial contributions. While the sale of indulgences was not new, Innocent VIII expanded this practice to generate massive revenues for both the Church and his family. Indulgences were often sold to wealthy individuals who sought to avoid the penalties of sin, essentially turning spiritual forgiveness into a commodity that could be purchased.

Innocent VIII's aggressive promotion of indulgences reflected his need to fund his family's lavish lifestyle and secure their political influence. His son, Franceschetto Cybo, was one of the primary beneficiaries of these funds, as the wealth generated through indulgences allowed him to pay off his gambling debts and maintain his luxurious existence. The Church's willingness to sell spiritual forgiveness for monetary gain during Innocent VIII's reign deepened the perception that the papacy had become hopelessly corrupt and disconnected from its spiritual mission.

This financial exploitation also extended to the broader Church administration, where Innocent VIII imposed **taxes on the clergy** and sought new ways to generate income from religious offices and duties. His financial policies prioritized enriching the Cybo family at the expense of the Church's moral authority, and his legacy was one of deepening distrust between the papacy and the faithful.

Nepotism and Familial Enrichment: One of the defining features of Innocent VIII's papacy was his blatant **nepotism**, as he used the power of his office to advance the interests of his illegitimate children and other family members. His son, Franceschetto Cybo, became the most notorious example of this nepotism, benefiting from his father's willingness to use church resources for personal gain. Innocent VIII provided Franceschetto with vast amounts of wealth, land, and titles, despite Franceschetto's reputation as a gambler and spendthrift.

The most significant example of Innocent VIII's nepotism was his **arranged marriage** between Franceschetto and **Maddalena de' Medici**, the daughter of **Lorenzo de' Medici**, one of the most powerful political figures in Renaissance Italy. This marriage cemented an alliance between the Cybo and Medici families, further consolidating Franceschetto's power and influence. However, the public saw this as yet another example of how Innocent VIII was using his position for personal and familial enrichment rather than focusing on his spiritual duties as pope.

Innocent VIII also worked to ensure that other members of the Cybo family were placed in key positions of power. He appointed relatives to prominent church offices and granted them lucrative estates, solidifying the Cybo family's influence across Italy. His reliance on nepotism damaged the Church's reputation and fueled growing concerns that the papacy had become more concerned with dynastic power and wealth than with guiding the faithful.

Political Alliances and Corruption: Innocent VIII's papacy was also marked by corrupt political alliances, particularly his close ties to **King Ferdinand I of Naples**. In exchange for Ferdinand's political support, Innocent VIII sought to secure wealth and power for the Cybo family. This included securing land and financial backing for his son Franceschetto, further entrenching the perception that Innocent's papacy was motivated by self-interest.

In return for political favors, Innocent VIII often turned a blind eye to the abuses of his allies, allowing corruption to flourish within both the Church and secular governments. His ability to navigate the complex political landscape of Italy during this time came at the cost of the Church's moral standing, as his alliances were often seen as opportunistic and driven by personal gain.

Impact on the Church and Legacy: Innocent VIII's corruption and nepotism had a profound impact on the Church's moral authority. His selling of church offices, indulgences, and political favors created widespread disillusionment among both the clergy and the laity, contributing to a growing sense that the papacy had lost its spiritual integrity. The financial exploitation and nepotism that defined Innocent VIII's reign also contributed to a broader crisis of faith within the Church, as people increasingly saw the Church as a corrupt institution focused on enriching its leaders rather than serving the faithful.

The corruption of Innocent VIII's papacy set the stage for the reforms that would follow in the early 16th century, as growing calls for change eventually led to the Protestant Reformation. His legacy remains one of moral compromise and familial enrichment, overshadowed by the scandals and financial exploitation that defined his reign.

In conclusion, Pope Innocent VIII's papacy was deeply marked by corruption, including the sale of church offices and indulgences, as well as the blatant use of papal power to enrich his family. His reliance on nepotism and financial exploitation severely damaged the Church's reputation and contributed to the moral decline that characterized the papacy during the late 15th century. While Innocent VIII's actions were not unique among Renaissance popes, his focus on enriching the Cybo family left a lasting stain on the Church's legacy, highlighting the extent to which personal gain and corruption had permeated the highest levels of ecclesiastical authority.

Handling His Family

POPE INNOCENT VIII'S papacy is widely known for the **nepotism** that permeated his reign, especially in how he managed the affairs of his children. Innocent VIII, born **Giovanni Battista Cybo**, had several illegitimate children, the most prominent being **Franceschetto Cybo** and **Teodorina Cybo**, whose lives and social standing he carefully orchestrated through a series of **advantageous marriages** and the strategic use of his papal power. Innocent VIII's focus on elevating his children's status through political and matrimonial alliances played a key role in shaping the perception of his papacy as more concerned with personal and familial advancement than with spiritual leadership.

Franceschetto Cybo: The Medici Alliance

Franceschetto Cybo, Innocent VIII's most prominent child, was a well-known figure during his father's papacy. Despite his reputation as a gambler and spendthrift, Innocent VIII used his influence as pope to secure Franceschetto's future and enhance the Cybo family's political standing. The centerpiece of Innocent VIII's strategy was his orchestration of Franceschetto's **marriage to Maddalena de' Medici**, the daughter of **Lorenzo de' Medici**, one of the most powerful political figures in Renaissance Italy.

This marriage, arranged in **1487**, was highly advantageous for both families. For Innocent VIII, the union gave the Cybo family a direct connection to the **Medici**, one of the most influential families in Italy, which bolstered his family's status and secured their future in the complex political landscape of the time. For the Medici, marrying into the pope's family offered enhanced influence within the Church and strengthened their political reach across Italy.

Innocent VIII spared no expense in ensuring that the marriage between Franceschetto and Maddalena was a grand affair, demonstrating the power and wealth of the Cybo family. The marriage brought Franceschetto substantial wealth, including land and titles, further consolidating his position in Italian society. Despite Franceschetto's personal flaws, the alliance with the Medici solidified the Cybo family's standing and ensured that they would be well-connected in both Church and secular affairs for generations to come.

Teodorina Cybo: Strategic Marriages and Alliances

Innocent VIII also used the strategy of marriage to advance the status of his daughter, **Teodorina Cybo**. Teodorina played a quieter role than her brother, but her marriage was equally important in cementing the Cybo family's influence. Innocent VIII arranged for Teodorina to marry **Gerardo Usodimare**, a member of a prominent Genoese noble family. This marriage helped the Cybo family strengthen their ties to Genoa, where they had long-standing roots.

Teodorina's marriage was another example of how Innocent VIII utilized his papal power to forge political alliances that benefited his family. By aligning with the Usodimare family, Innocent VIII ensured that the Cybo family maintained influence in northern Italy and consolidated their noble status. This marriage, like Franceschetto's, was a deliberate move to ensure that Innocent VIII's children remained prominent in Italian political and social circles, further demonstrating the extent to which his papacy was focused on familial advancement.

Papal Power and Family Advancement

Throughout his papacy, Innocent VIII used his **ecclesiastical authority** and political influence to elevate his family's status. He appointed relatives to high-ranking Church positions, granted them control over vast estates, and ensured that they enjoyed a privileged status in both Church and secular affairs. Franceschetto, in particular, was granted large sums of money and titles, despite his known personal shortcomings, highlighting Innocent's willingness to use papal resources to benefit his family.

In addition to arranging advantageous marriages, Innocent VIII's use of **nepotism** extended to granting Franceschetto control over several **Church offices**, which allowed him to accumulate significant wealth. Innocent VIII's papacy was defined by his efforts to secure power and privilege for his children, often at the expense of the Church's moral standing. The pope's ability to use his position to enrich his family was a common practice among Renaissance popes, but Innocent VIII's actions were particularly notable due to the scale of his nepotism.

Impact of Nepotism on Innocent VIII's Papacy

Innocent VIII's focus on promoting his family through strategic marriages and nepotism had a significant impact on the perception of his papacy. His actions were widely criticized for contributing to the growing sense of **corruption** within the Church, as many viewed his use of papal power to benefit his children as evidence that the papacy had become more concerned with secular and dynastic matters than with spiritual leadership.

While the marriage alliances that Innocent VIII arranged for his children brought considerable advantages to the Cybo family, they also deepened the perception that the papacy was mired in nepotism and self-interest. Innocent's willingness to leverage Church offices, indulgences, and resources to secure his children's future demonstrated the extent to which the Renaissance papacy had become entangled in the pursuit of power and wealth.

In conclusion, Innocent VIII's handling of his family, particularly through the strategic marriages of his children Franceschetto and Teodorina, was a defining feature of his papacy. By arranging advantageous alliances with powerful families such as the **Medici** and **Usodimare**, Innocent VIII secured the Cybo family's prominence in Italian politics and society. However, his blatant nepotism and use of papal resources for personal gain also contributed to the growing disillusionment with the papacy, reinforcing the perception of corruption that would fuel future calls for reform within the Church.

9. Pope Alexander VI (1492–1503)

Life and Background

Pope Alexander VI, born **Rodrigo de Borja (Borgia)** on **January 1, 1431**, in **Xàtiva**, Spain, was one of the most controversial and infamous popes in the history of the Catholic Church. His papacy, marked by scandal, corruption, and the open promotion of his family's power, epitomized the excesses of the Renaissance papacy. Before ascending to the papal throne, Rodrigo Borgia lived a life filled with ambition, securing a place for his family in the politics of both the Church and Italy. His numerous children, especially **Cesare Borgia** and **Lucrezia Borgia**, played significant roles during his papacy, and their actions contributed to the enduring legacy of the **Borgia** family as symbols of power, intrigue, and moral corruption.

Early Life and Rise to Power: Rodrigo Borgia was born into a noble Spanish family with connections to the papacy through his uncle, **Pope Callixtus III**, who elevated the Borgia family's fortunes when he became pope in 1455. With the help of his uncle, Rodrigo quickly ascended through the ranks of the Church, securing powerful positions, including **cardinal** in 1456 and **vice-chancellor of the Church**, a position that gave him control over significant financial resources. His skill as a diplomat, administrator, and politician earned him favor among the curia, but his reputation for corruption, including **bribery** and **simony**, grew alongside his power.

Rodrigo's reputation for enjoying the pleasures of life also became well-known. He had several **mistresses** over the years, and his relationships resulted in a large number of illegitimate children, most of whom he openly acknowledged and used to strengthen his family's political position. Despite his controversial personal life, Rodrigo Borgia was elected **Pope Alexander VI** in **1492** after securing support from influential cardinals, allegedly through heavy bribery, further cementing his reputation for corruption.

Cesare Borgia: One of Alexander VI's most famous and notorious children was **Cesare Borgia**, born in **1475** to Rodrigo and his long-term mistress **Vannozza dei Cattanei**. Initially destined for a career in the Church, Cesare was appointed **cardinal** at a young age, but he quickly grew disillusioned with religious life and desired power on the battlefield and in politics. In **1498**, Cesare renounced his position in the Church and became a **condottiero** (military leader), pursuing his ambition of establishing a **Borgia dynasty** in Italy.

With the full backing of his father, Cesare sought to carve out a principality for himself in central Italy. Alexander VI used his papal power to grant Cesare titles and military support, including forging alliances with powerful European rulers like **King Louis XII of France**. Cesare's ruthlessness, strategic brilliance, and political cunning made him both feared and admired by his contemporaries. His military campaigns to conquer Italian territories, especially in the **Romagna**, were marked by a mixture of diplomacy and brutality, and he became a model for **Machiavelli's** famous treatise *The Prince*.

Cesare's ambitions were inseparable from his father's papacy, as Pope Alexander VI funneled Church resources into supporting Cesare's military conquests and political machinations. Cesare's role as the primary enforcer of the Borgia family's power, coupled with his father's use of the papacy for personal and dynastic gain, cemented the Borgia family's infamy.

Lucrezia Borgia: Another of Alexander VI's most well-known children was **Lucrezia Borgia**, born in **1480** to Rodrigo Borgia and Vannozza dei Cattanei. While Lucrezia's reputation has often been tainted by rumors of scandal, including accusations of **incest** and **poisoning**, modern historians have begun to reevaluate her role, seeing her more as a victim of political manipulation than an active participant in the darker deeds associated with the Borgia family.

Lucrezia's marriages were strategic alliances orchestrated by her father and brother to strengthen the Borgia family's political influence. Her first marriage to **Giovanni Sforza** in **1493** allied the Borgias with the powerful **Sforza family** of Milan, but when the alliance no longer served the family's interests, the marriage was annulled. Lucrezia's subsequent marriages followed a similar pattern, each one crafted to advance the Borgia family's position in Italy. Her second marriage to **Alfonso of Aragon** was more politically advantageous, connecting the Borgia family to the **Kingdom of Naples**, but it ended in tragedy when Alfonso was murdered, allegedly on the orders of Cesare.

Despite the scandals surrounding her, Lucrezia was known for her intelligence, beauty, and administrative skills. During her third marriage to **Alfonso d'Este**, the Duke of Ferrara, Lucrezia became a respected figure in the Ferrara court and helped improve the family's reputation. Her role as a **diplomat** and patron of the arts in Ferrara allowed her to distance herself from the shadow of the Borgia scandals, and she became an influential figure in Renaissance Italy.

Other Borgia Children: In addition to Cesare and Lucrezia, Pope Alexander VI had several other children who were also involved in the political machinations of the Borgia family. Among them was **Giovanni Borgia**, also known as **Juan**, who was made **Duke of Gandía**. Juan's violent death in **1497** remains shrouded in mystery, with rumors suggesting that he was murdered on the orders of his brother Cesare, though this has never been proven.

Rodrigo also had other children, such as **Gioffre Borgia**, who married into the **Naples royal family** as part of his father's efforts to secure political alliances throughout Italy. Like his siblings, Gioffre's marriage was arranged to strengthen the family's influence, though he did not play as prominent a role as Cesare or Lucrezia in the Borgia's broader ambitions.

The Borgia Legacy: Pope Alexander VI's papacy was defined by his use of **Church resources** and his position as pope to promote and secure his family's interests. His numerous children, particularly Cesare and Lucrezia, were central to his political strategy, as he sought to expand the Borgia family's power and create a dynasty that would rule over parts of Italy. While Alexander VI's reign brought short-term success for the Borgia family, it also left a legacy of **scandal**, **corruption**, and moral decay that tainted the reputation of the papacy for years to come.

In conclusion, Pope Alexander VI's life and background were inextricably tied to his efforts to elevate his children, Cesare and Lucrezia Borgia, to positions of power and influence. His papacy was marked by scandalous behavior, from using the Church to enrich his family to orchestrating political marriages for his children. The Borgia legacy remains one of the most infamous in Church history, with Cesare and Lucrezia symbolizing the ambition and intrigue that defined the Borgia family's rise to power under the watchful eye of Pope Alexander VI.

Scandals and Exploits

POPE ALEXANDER VI, born **Rodrigo Borgia**, is remembered as one of the most scandalous and controversial popes in the history of the Catholic Church. His papacy, rife with accusations of **corruption**, **nepotism**, **favoritism**, and **debauchery**, marked the height of the **Renaissance papacy's** excesses. Alexander VI's blatant use of his position to enrich and promote his family, combined with his open relationships with **mistresses** and personal indulgences, made him a notorious figure both during and after his reign.

Relationships with Mistresses: One of the most widely known scandals surrounding Alexander VI was his numerous **open relationships** with mistresses, which was highly unusual for a pope, who was expected to lead a life of celibacy and moral virtue. Rodrigo Borgia fathered several **illegitimate children** by his mistresses, most notably his long-term lover **Vannozza dei Cattanei**, with whom he had four children: **Cesare**, **Lucrezia**, **Giovanni**, and **Gioffre**. These children were openly acknowledged by Rodrigo, and he made little effort to hide his relationships, a clear violation of the celibacy expected of clergy.

In addition to Vannozza, Alexander VI had affairs with other women, including the much younger **Giulia Farnese**, who became his mistress during his papacy. Giulia, known for her beauty, was married to **Orsino Orsini**, but she spent much of her time in the Vatican as Alexander's lover. The fact that the pope openly kept a mistress at the papal court further fueled accusations of moral corruption and decadence. Giulia's presence at the Vatican, and the power and influence she wielded due to her relationship with Alexander VI, became a source of gossip and scandal across Rome and beyond.

The open nature of Alexander VI's relationships and his fathering of children while serving as pope was unprecedented. While other popes had engaged in similar behavior in private, Alexander's public flaunting of his mistresses and children shocked many within the Church and contributed to the image of the papacy as corrupt and morally compromised during the Renaissance.

Favoritism Toward His Children: Perhaps the most significant scandal of Alexander VI's papacy was his **blatant favoritism** toward his children, whom he openly acknowledged and promoted during his reign. The most notorious of these children were **Cesare Borgia** and **Lucrezia Borgia**, both of whom benefited immensely from their father's power and influence.

Cesare Borgia, initially made a cardinal at a young age, was allowed to leave the Church to pursue a military and political career. Alexander VI used his position as pope to provide Cesare with titles, land, and military resources, allowing him to carve out a **Borgia-controlled territory** in central Italy. Cesare's ruthless military campaigns, backed by papal resources, helped him become one of the most feared and powerful figures in Italy, but his rise was inseparable from the blatant nepotism practiced by his father.

Alexander VI also arranged advantageous marriages for **Lucrezia Borgia**, which were designed to strengthen the family's political alliances. Lucrezia's marriages were seen as strategic moves to further the Borgia family's influence, and her role in these alliances contributed to the perception of the family as politically cunning and manipulative. Lucrezia's personal life was the subject of much rumor and scandal, including accusations of **incest** with her father and brother, although modern historians largely regard these claims as exaggerations or fabrications by political enemies.

Alexander VI's favoritism toward his children extended beyond providing them with titles and wealth; he used the power of the papacy itself to ensure their dominance in the Italian political landscape. His papal decrees were often aimed at protecting and advancing the Borgia family's interests, a clear violation of the spiritual mission of the

Church. His willingness to compromise the papacy for personal and familial gain further tarnished the moral authority of the Church.

Nepotism and Corruption: Alexander VI's papacy was notorious for its **nepotism**, as he frequently appointed his relatives and loyal supporters to key positions within the Church and secular governments. This nepotism not only enriched the Borgia family but also ensured that they held sway over the politics of Italy and beyond. Alexander VI's ability to manipulate the Church's resources for his family's benefit led to widespread accusations of **simony**—the buying and selling of Church offices.

One of the most significant examples of this nepotism was Alexander VI's promotion of **Cardinal Alessandro Farnese**, the brother of his mistress Giulia Farnese, to high-ranking positions within the Church. Alessandro Farnese, who later became **Pope Paul III**, owed much of his early success to the influence of his sister's relationship with the pope. This blatant favoritism in appointing relatives to key Church roles further demonstrated Alexander's willingness to use the papal office for personal advantage.

Alexander VI's corrupt practices extended to the **selling of indulgences** and other ecclesiastical privileges in exchange for financial support. The funds raised through these practices were often diverted to the Borgia family's coffers or used to finance Cesare Borgia's military campaigns. This financial exploitation of the Church's resources contributed to the widespread perception that the papacy under Alexander VI was driven by greed and self-interest rather than spiritual leadership.

Political Manipulations and Power Struggles: Alexander VI was deeply involved in the political machinations of Italy, using the papacy to further his ambitions of creating a **Borgia dynasty**. He forged alliances with powerful rulers, including **King Charles VIII of France**, and was skilled in playing rival factions against each other to ensure his family's dominance. His ability to navigate the complex political landscape of Italy allowed him to strengthen the Borgia family's position, but it also embroiled the papacy in numerous conflicts and controversies.

One of the most notorious episodes of Alexander VI's political career was his **alliance with King Louis XII of France** in exchange for French military support for Cesare Borgia's campaigns in Italy. In return, Alexander annulled Louis XII's marriage, allowing the French king to remarry and secure his claim to the throne. This blatant use of papal authority to manipulate secular politics further damaged the reputation of the Church.

Alexander VI's political manipulations often came at a high cost. His papacy was marked by constant power struggles with other Italian families, including the **Orsini** and the **Colonna**, as well as with foreign powers seeking influence in Italy. These conflicts weakened the papacy's spiritual authority and reinforced the perception that the pope was more concerned with temporal power than with guiding the faithful.

Legacy of Scandal and Infamy: The legacy of Pope Alexander VI is one of **scandal**, **corruption**, and **moral decadence**. His open relationships with mistresses, his blatant favoritism toward his children, and his willingness to compromise the spiritual mission of the papacy for personal gain made him one of the most controversial figures in Church history. The actions of Alexander VI and his children, particularly Cesare and Lucrezia Borgia, became synonymous with the excesses of the Renaissance papacy and contributed to the growing calls for **reform** that would eventually culminate in the **Protestant Reformation**.

In conclusion, Pope Alexander VI's papacy was defined by numerous scandals and exploits, including his open relationships with mistresses, his notorious favoritism toward his children, and his use of the papal office for personal and familial gain. His legacy remains one of the most infamous in the history of the Catholic Church, symbolizing the corruption and moral decline that characterized the Renaissance papacy.

Corruption

POPE ALEXANDER VI, born **Rodrigo Borgia**, is one of the most infamous popes in history due to his **blatant corruption** and manipulation of the papacy to **enrich and empower his family**. His use of nepotism, simony, and political intrigue allowed his children and relatives to rise to positions of great influence in the Church and across European politics. Alexander VI's actions exemplified the excesses of the Renaissance papacy, where personal ambition often eclipsed spiritual leadership, and the highest office in the Church became a tool for dynastic and political maneuvering.

Nepotism and Family Advancement: One of the hallmarks of Alexander VI's papacy was his extensive use of **nepotism** to benefit his family, particularly his children. Although born out of wedlock, his children were openly acknowledged and favored, with Alexander using his papal authority to place them in powerful positions. His most notorious children, **Cesare** and **Lucrezia Borgia**, benefited immensely from his actions, gaining influence in both ecclesiastical and secular realms.

Alexander VI appointed his son **Cesare Borgia** as a **cardinal** at a young age, even though Cesare had little interest in religious life. The appointment was not based on merit or spiritual devotion but was a clear example of the pope using the Church to enhance his family's status. However, Cesare's true ambitions lay in military and political power, and Alexander VI eventually released him from his ecclesiastical duties, allowing Cesare to pursue his career as a **condottiero** (military leader). With his father's backing, Cesare launched a series of military campaigns to carve out a **Borgia-controlled state** in central Italy. These efforts were funded in large part by the wealth of the Church, with Alexander VI using papal resources to support his son's ambitions.

Lucrezia Borgia, Alexander's daughter, was also a key figure in the pope's plans to solidify the family's influence. Through a series of

strategic marriages arranged by her father, Lucrezia became a pawn in the Borgia family's political machinations. Her marriages to powerful noblemen were designed to form alliances that would benefit the Borgia family's standing in Italy. While Lucrezia's role was largely diplomatic, her position as the daughter of the pope allowed her to wield considerable influence, both within the papal court and in the noble families of Italy.

Simony and Selling Church Offices: Another major aspect of Alexander VI's corruption was his involvement in **simony**, the practice of selling Church offices and positions for personal gain. During his papacy, Alexander VI openly sold positions within the Church hierarchy to the highest bidder, regardless of the candidates' qualifications or spiritual commitment. This practice not only enriched the pope and his family but also undermined the integrity of the Church, as key ecclesiastical positions were filled by those who could afford them rather than by individuals committed to serving the faithful.

One of the most notorious examples of this corruption was Alexander VI's appointment of **Cardinal Alessandro Farnese**, the brother of his mistress **Giulia Farnese**, to prominent positions within the Church. Alessandro Farnese's rise through the Church hierarchy was not based on merit but on his family's connection to the Borgia pope. This blatant favoritism and exchange of power for financial or personal gain contributed to the perception of the papacy as morally bankrupt.

The selling of indulgences, Church lands, and ecclesiastical privileges was also a common practice under Alexander VI's reign. He used these financial resources to enrich the Borgia family and fund Cesare's military campaigns, further entangling the spiritual mission of the Church with personal and political ambition. Alexander VI's willingness to exploit the wealth of the Church for personal gain deepened the perception that the papacy had become little more than a tool for dynastic power rather than a seat of religious authority.

Political Manipulation and International Influence: Alexander VI's papacy was also marked by his shrewd manipulation of European politics to further the interests of the Borgia family. His alliances with powerful rulers and states were often motivated by the desire to strengthen his family's hold on Italy and increase their influence across Europe.

One of the most significant political maneuvers was Alexander VI's **alliance with King Charles VIII of France**. In exchange for French support of Cesare's campaigns in Italy, Alexander VI offered Charles political concessions and facilitated his invasion of the Kingdom of Naples. This alliance, though beneficial to the Borgia family in the short term, embroiled the papacy in the complex and often bloody power struggles of the Italian Wars, further diminishing the spiritual authority of the Church.

Alexander VI's political maneuvering also extended to other European powers. He aligned himself with **Ferdinand of Aragon** and **Isabella of Castile**, issuing the **papal bull Inter Caetera** in 1493, which granted Spain rights to the lands discovered by Christopher Columbus in the New World. This decision further cemented the pope's influence in international affairs and demonstrated how he used his position to gain favor with European monarchs while also advancing his family's interests.

The Impact of Cesare Borgia: Much of Alexander VI's papacy revolved around advancing the political and military career of **Cesare Borgia**, his most ambitious child. Cesare's goal of creating a **Borgia dynasty** in Italy was largely enabled by his father's use of the papal office to provide him with financial and military support. Alexander VI granted Cesare titles, lands, and papal armies, allowing him to conquer territories in **Romagna** and central Italy.

Cesare's military campaigns were brutal, and his methods of consolidating power—through assassination, bribery, and political manipulation—became notorious throughout Italy. His ruthless ambition and the wealth and power granted to him by his father made him one of the most feared and powerful figures in Italy. However, his rise was inseparable from Alexander VI's willingness to use papal resources for personal and familial gain, further entrenching the perception of the Borgia family as corrupt and power-hungry.

Public Perception and Legacy: Alexander VI's corruption and favoritism toward his family had profound consequences for the Church and its reputation. His papacy became a symbol of the **moral decay** that had taken hold of the Renaissance papacy, where spiritual authority was overshadowed by political intrigue, personal ambition, and financial exploitation. The blatant nepotism practiced by Alexander VI, combined with his use of Church offices and resources to enrich his family, led to widespread disillusionment with the papacy.

The legacy of Alexander VI's papacy was one of scandal and infamy, with the **Borgia name** becoming synonymous with corruption, intrigue, and debauchery. His actions contributed to the growing sense of dissatisfaction with the Church, fueling the calls for reform that would eventually lead to the **Protestant Reformation** in the early 16th century.

In conclusion, Pope Alexander VI's use of his position to benefit his family—through nepotism, simony, and political manipulation—stands as one of the most notorious examples of corruption in the history of the papacy. His actions not only enriched the Borgia family and strengthened their influence over European politics but also contributed to the moral decline of the Church, leaving a lasting stain on the reputation of the papacy.

Handling His Family

POPE ALEXANDER VI, born **Rodrigo Borgia**, is notorious for using his papal power to maneuver his children into positions of great influence and power, treating the papacy as a personal tool for building a **Borgia dynasty**. His blatant nepotism shaped much of his papacy, as he positioned his son, **Cesare Borgia**, to become a powerful military leader and arranged advantageous marriages for his daughter, **Lucrezia Borgia**, to forge political alliances. Through these actions, Alexander VI ensured that his children played pivotal roles in both Italian and European politics, intertwining the papacy with his family's ambitions.

Cesare Borgia: From Cardinal to Military Leader

Initially, Alexander VI sought to secure his son **Cesare Borgia** within the Church hierarchy, making him a **cardinal** in **1493**, despite Cesare's young age and lack of religious vocation. The appointment was not motivated by Cesare's devotion to the Church but by Alexander VI's desire to consolidate power within the Borgia family. However, Cesare's ambitions soon surpassed his role in the Church, as he aspired to pursue a career in **military leadership** and territorial conquest.

In **1498**, with the backing of his father, Cesare resigned from his position as cardinal—the first time in history that a cardinal had renounced his ecclesiastical title. Alexander VI then orchestrated Cesare's transition into a political and military career, securing a **duchy in France** by arranging his marriage to **Charlotte d'Albret**, a member of the French royal family. This marriage not only allied the Borgia family with France but also provided Cesare with the resources and political connections he needed to launch his military campaigns.

With Alexander VI's support, Cesare began his quest to carve out a **Borgia-controlled state** in central Italy. Using papal funds and military support, Cesare conquered several territories in the **Romagna** region, including **Imola**, **Forlì**, and **Rimini**. Alexander VI used his papal authority to grant Cesare the title of **Duke of Romagna** and ensured that papal armies and resources were at Cesare's disposal. Cesare's military campaigns were brutal and efficient, and his ruthlessness earned him both fear and admiration. His father's support was crucial in allowing him to become one of the most powerful condottieri (military leaders) in Italy.

Cesare's rise to power was inseparable from his father's manipulation of the papal office. Alexander VI's willingness to use Church wealth and influence to further Cesare's ambitions exemplified his determination to establish a **Borgia dynasty** that would rival the other noble families of Italy. Through Cesare, Alexander VI sought to create a legacy of territorial control and political dominance for the Borgia family, even if it meant compromising the spiritual integrity of the papacy.

Lucrezia Borgia: Strategic Marriages and Political Alliances

Alexander VI also used his daughter, **Lucrezia Borgia**, as a key pawn in his political strategies, arranging a series of **strategic marriages** that were designed to forge alliances and strengthen the Borgia family's influence across Italy. Lucrezia's beauty, intelligence, and charm made her an attractive candidate for marriage alliances, and Alexander VI sought to leverage her marriages to secure the family's position.

Lucrezia's first marriage was to **Giovanni Sforza** in **1493**, a member of the powerful **Sforza family** of Milan. This marriage was intended to secure an alliance between the Borgias and the Sforzas, two of the most influential families in Italy at the time. However, when the alliance became politically inconvenient for Alexander VI, he orchestrated the annulment of the marriage in **1497**, claiming that Giovanni was impotent—an allegation that humiliated Giovanni and damaged his reputation.

Lucrezia's second marriage was to **Alfonso of Aragon**, the illegitimate son of the King of Naples, in **1498**. This marriage was meant to strengthen the Borgia family's ties to the **Kingdom of**

Naples, another key power in Italy. However, this alliance proved short-lived, as Alfonso was murdered in **1500** under mysterious circumstances, with rumors circulating that Cesare had orchestrated the assassination to further his political ambitions. Alfonso's death eliminated a potential rival to Cesare's growing power, further entrenching the Borgia family's control over Italian politics.

Lucrezia's third and most significant marriage was to **Alfonso d'Este**, the Duke of Ferrara, in **1501**. This marriage was one of the most prestigious alliances arranged by Alexander VI, as it aligned the Borgia family with one of the most important noble families in northern Italy. The **Este family** was highly respected, and Lucrezia's marriage to Alfonso helped rehabilitate her image, which had been tainted by rumors of scandal and intrigue. As Duchess of Ferrara, Lucrezia became a respected figure, known for her patronage of the arts and her diplomatic skills. She managed to distance herself from the darker aspects of the Borgia legacy, establishing herself as a prominent figure in the **Ferrara court**.

Through these marriages, Alexander VI positioned Lucrezia as a key diplomatic figure, using her relationships to secure alliances that would benefit the Borgia family. Her marriages were not about personal choice but about political strategy, and Alexander VI's ability to maneuver her into these unions demonstrated his skill in using familial connections to advance his ambitions.

The Borgia Family as a Political Power

Under Alexander VI's leadership, the Borgia family became one of the most powerful and feared dynasties in Italy. His handling of Cesare and Lucrezia, in particular, showed how he used the papacy to secure political power for his family, treating the Church not as a spiritual institution but as a **political machine**. Alexander VI's papacy was marked by a relentless focus on family advancement, with every move calculated to ensure that the Borgia name would dominate Italian politics for years to come.

The **strategic marriages** of Lucrezia and the **military career** of Cesare were essential components of Alexander VI's broader plan to create a **Borgia-controlled state** in Italy. His willingness to compromise the spiritual integrity of the Church in pursuit of these goals earned him widespread condemnation, and his actions contributed to the perception of the papacy as corrupt and morally bankrupt.

Conclusion

Pope Alexander VI's manipulation of his children's lives to secure their political and military power was a defining feature of his papacy. By maneuvering Cesare into a position of military leadership and arranging strategic marriages for Lucrezia, Alexander VI used the papal office to advance the Borgia family's ambitions, intertwining the fate of the Church with that of his family. His actions not only entrenched the Borgia family's influence but also contributed to the broader decline of the papacy's moral authority, leaving a legacy of scandal and corruption that would shape perceptions of the Church for generations.

Conclusion

As we reach the conclusion of this exploration into the lives, scandals, and corruptions of the popes who used their papal power to benefit their families, it's clear that the history of the papacy is as complex and multifaceted as the individuals who held the title of Pope. The infamous stories of **Pope Innocent VIII, Pope Alexander VI**, and others reveal a time when the papal office was deeply intertwined with the secular ambitions of noble families, turning the Vatican into a hub of **nepotism**, **political intrigue**, and **moral compromise**. While these popes held the highest spiritual office in the Christian world, their actions often reflected the very human desires for power, wealth, and legacy.

The popes featured in this book were products of the **Renaissance**, an era that blurred the lines between spiritual and temporal authority. As leaders of the Catholic Church, they were expected to uphold Christian morality and provide spiritual guidance to millions. Yet, as men born into the dynastic struggles of Italy and Europe, they often succumbed to the same political machinations and personal indulgences that characterized the noble families of the time. Their use of **church offices, marriages**, and even the military to advance their family interests not only altered the course of history but also profoundly shaped the perception of the papacy as an institution capable of both great influence and deep corruption.

The Scandal of Nepotism and Family Power

Throughout the chapters of this book, we have seen how popes like **Innocent VIII** and **Alexander VI** brazenly promoted their children, granting them lands, titles, and influence within the Church and across Europe. The papacy, under these popes, became an instrument of **dynastic ambition**, as family members were maneuvered into positions of power to secure a lasting legacy. Innocent VIII's promotion of his son **Franceschetto Cybo**, and Alexander VI's relentless efforts to advance **Cesare** and **Lucrezia Borgia**, are emblematic of this era of papal history.

This use of the Church for personal gain exposed the papacy to widespread criticism and scandal, both from within the clergy and among the faithful. Popes like Alexander VI, with their open relationships with mistresses and unabashed pursuit of power for their children, contributed to the growing belief that the Church was morally bankrupt. This disillusionment with the papacy, compounded by the increasing corruption within the Vatican, played a key role in the calls for reform that would eventually culminate in the **Protestant Reformation.**

Power, Corruption, and the Legacy of the Renaissance Papacy

While the popes featured in this book represent some of the most notorious examples of papal corruption, their actions also reflect the larger context of the **Renaissance.** This was a time when power was consolidated through familial alliances, political marriages, and the accumulation of wealth and influence. The Church, as one of the most powerful institutions in Europe, was not immune to these forces. In fact, the papacy became a central player in the power struggles of Italy and beyond, with popes acting as both spiritual leaders and political rulers.

The scandals of the Borgia family, particularly under **Pope Alexander VI**, encapsulate this dynamic. Alexander's ability to manipulate both the spiritual and political spheres to benefit his children, Cesare and Lucrezia, is perhaps the most famous example of how the papal office was used for personal gain. Cesare's ruthless campaigns to establish a **Borgia-controlled state** and Lucrezia's politically strategic marriages were key to Alexander VI's vision of a lasting dynasty. However, their rise to power also sowed the seeds of the Borgia family's eventual downfall, as their enemies in Italy and Europe turned against them.

The Unholy Unions: A Study in Papal Corruption

At the heart of this book is the exploration of the **unholy unions** formed between popes, their families, and the political systems of their time. These popes' relationships with their children, mistresses, and political allies highlight the extent to which the papal office could be compromised by personal ambition. The stories of popes like **John XII**, **Benedict IX**, **Innocent VIII**, and **Alexander VI** reveal a papacy at the height of its temporal power but at the expense of its spiritual authority.

This book does not merely chronicle the moral failings of these popes but also seeks to understand how and why the papacy became so deeply entangled in the secular affairs of the Renaissance. The actions of these popes were, in many ways, symptomatic of the broader culture of **corruption** and **dynastic ambition** that defined the politics of 15th- and 16th-century Italy. While their behavior may seem shocking from a modern perspective, it reflects the realities of a time when power and influence were the ultimate currency.

The Need for Reform and the Aftermath

The corrupt practices of popes like Alexander VI did not go unchallenged. As this book has demonstrated, the excesses of the Renaissance papacy ultimately led to widespread calls for **reform**. The moral decay and blatant nepotism of these popes contributed to the rising tide of dissatisfaction that would culminate in the **Protestant Reformation** and the **Council of Trent**. The papacy would eventually undergo significant reforms in the 16th century, as the Catholic Church sought to address the very issues of corruption and abuse of power that had come to define it during the Renaissance.

In conclusion, this book has offered a detailed look at the lives of some of the most notorious popes in history, exploring how they used their spiritual authority to pursue personal and familial gain. From **selling church offices** to promoting illegitimate children, these popes shaped the political landscape of Europe and left an indelible mark on the history of the Church. Their legacies, while stained by scandal, provide a window into an era when the boundaries between spiritual and secular power were blurred, and the papacy became a symbol of both immense influence and profound corruption.